pies & tarts

pies & tarts

simple recipes for delicious food every day

RYLAND PETERS & SMALL

LONDON • NEW YORK

Designer Emily Breen

Commissioning Editor Nathan Joyce

Production Controller Meskerem Berhane

Art Director Leslie Harrington

Editorial Director Julia Charles

First published in 2014 by
Ryland Peters & Small
20–21 Jockey's Fields
London WC1R 4BW
and
519 Broadway, 5th Floor
New York NY 10012

www.rylandpeters.com

Text © Jordan Bourke, Maxine Clark,
Julian Day, Ross Dobson, Hannah Miles,
Miisa Mink, Isidora Popovic, Laura
Washburn and Ryland Peters & Small
2014

Design and photographs © Ryland
Peters & Small 2014

ISBN: 978-1-84975-571-9

10 9 8 7 6 5 4 3 2 1

A CIP record for this book is available
from the British Library.

US Library of Congress Cataloging-in-
Publication data has been applied for.

Printed and bound in China

notes

• All spoon measurements are level,
unless otherwise specified.

• All herbs used in these recipes are
fresh, unless otherwise specified.

• All fruit and vegetables should be
washed thoroughly before
consumption. Unwaxed citrus fruits
should be used whenever possible.

• The recipes in this book are
given in both metric and imperial
measurements. However, the spellings
are primarily British.

• Eggs used in this book are UK large
and US extra large unless otherwise
specified. Recipes containing raw or
partially cooked egg should not be
served to the very young, very old,
anyone with a compromised immune
system or pregnant women.

contents

introduction

Who doesn't love a pie or a tart? Whether it be a hearty, nurturing Steak and Kidney Pie on a winter's day or a light Broccoli and Chorizo Tart for a summer picnic, a tangy and refreshing Tarte au Citron to share with friends or a good, old-fashioned Simple Apple Pie to enjoy on a Sunday with the family, there's something for all tastes and all occasions.

There's something so magical about a pie. Breaking the golden seal and feeling the rich aroma drift into your nostrils is heavenly enough, even before you dive into the secret filling below. Tarts are quicker and much less complicated to make than pies, as they aren't covered. They can be rustled up at very short notice, even if you haven't made the pastry already.

You'll find some useful tips in this book to ensure that your pies and tarts come out perfectly every time. For example, be sure that the filling isn't too wet or it will ooze out of the pastry and make it go soggy before it has time to crisp up nicely. Also, don't be scared to make your own pastry – with modern appliances like the food processor, bad pastry is a thing of the past. In this book, you'll find a handy section on basic pastry techniques and recipes. Once you've mastered them, you'll never look back!

This book is divided into six chapters: Basic Pastry, Savoury Pies, Sweet Pies, Savoury Tarts, Sweet Tarts and Party Pies and Tartlets. Most of these recipes are really easy to make, while a couple require a little more skill and patience. Before long you'll be experimenting and creating with your own inventive, flavoursome recipes!

For perfect results every time, follow these simple and effective recipes garnered from a lifetime of pastry and pie making. Read on and digest and you'll become a master pieman/woman!

basic pastry

techniques

Rolling the Pastry

- Pastry is easier to roll out if shaped into a ball, then flattened to a thick disk **(1)** before wrapping and chilling. Make sure you allow the pastry to soften slightly before rolling.
- Lightly dust a work surface with flour.
- To prevent sticking, flour your hands and the rolling pin rather than showering the pastry with extra flour – this will avoid a build-up of powdery flour on the pastry.
- When rolling pastry, keep it moving on a 'hovercraft' of flour and it will never stick. Or try rolling pastry directly onto a piece of non-stick parchment paper or clingfilm/plastic wrap – this allows it be moved around easily and it will not stick to the work surface. The pastry can also be easily lifted and laid over a pie or tart without it stretching.
- Hold the rolling pin at either end, place on the pastry dough and always roll directly away from you. Move the pastry around by short turns in one direction so that you roll it evenly **(2)**. Never flip the pastry over.
- Keep the rolling pin level for even thickness. Setting two chopsticks (or similar) on either side of the dough before rolling will help you to roll it out evenly to the thickness of the chopstick.
- Place your pie pan or dish on top of the rolled out pastry to check it is large enough to cover the surface **(3)**.

Don't forget to include the height of the sides in your calculations.

- Once the pastry is the right size and thickness, roll the flour-dusted pastry around the rolling pin to help you to pick it up **(4)** – this will avoid stretching the pastry and stop it shrinking when cooking.

Lining a Pie Pan or Dish

- Drape the pastry over the pan and work it into the corners, being careful not to tear the pastry **(5)**. (There is no need to grease a pie pan before lining, unless you have a vertical surface that you want the pastry to adhere to i.e. a deep loaf pan.)
- Use a small piece of extra pastry wrapped in a piece of clingfilm/plastic wrap to help to push the pastry into the edges of the pan **(6)**.
- To make a single-crust pie, press the pastry up the sides of the pan and cut off the overhang with a very sharp knife. Or use a rolling pin to roll over the top **(7)**, which will trim off any excess pastry very neatly **(8)**. (Don't trim the excess if making a double-crust pie – you will trim both crusts off together.) Chill or freeze before baking.

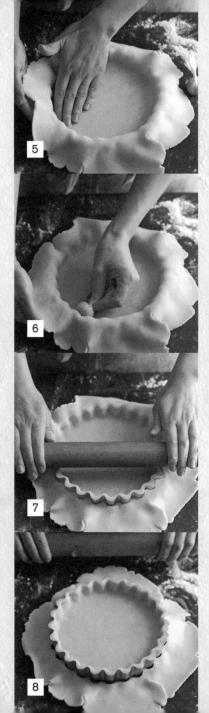

Baking blind

By 'baking blind', you pre-cook the pie crust so that it cooks through before the filling goes in and is less likely to become soggy. It also stops the pastry edges from collapsing into the filling.

• Prick the pie crust all over with a fork **(9)**.

• Line the pie crust with a piece of well-crumpled parchment paper or kitchen foil and fill with a layer of baking beans **(10)**.

• Bake the pastry at 200°C (400°F) Gas 6 for 15 minutes then remove from the oven and lift out the baking parchment or foil and baking beans **(11)**. Return to the oven and bake for a further 10 minutes or so until dried out, lightly golden and cooked through **(12)**. Leave to cool.

Filling the pie

• Once the pan is lined, spoon in the cold filling, being careful not to splash the edges or overfill so that the top will seal properly.

• If the filling is likely to collapse slightly as it cooks (this will happen if raw fruit or meat is put in the pie), insert a pie funnel before you add the pastry lid. This will help steam escape as well as holding the pastry up so it cooks evenly and doesn't collapse into the dish. This is particularly important when putting a single-crust lid onto a deep-dish pie – the pastry can easily slip off the edges and collapse into the filling.

• Cover and cook as soon as possible.

basic shortcrust pastry

This is the classic method for making short and crumbly shortcrust pastry It is made with half butter and half lard – the butter for flavour and the lard for shortness.

250 g/2 cups plain/all-purpose flour

a pinch of salt

50 g/3 tablespoons lard (or white cooking fat/shortening), chilled and diced

75 g/5 tablespoons unsalted butter, chilled and diced

2–3 tablespoons ice-cold water

Makes about 400 g/14 oz. (enough to line the base of a 23–25-cm/9–10-inch loose-based tart pan or make a double crust for a 20–23-cm/8–9-inch pie plate)

The Classic Way

Sift the flour and salt together into a large mixing bowl **(1)**.

Add the lard and butter **(2)** and rub in **(3)** until the mixture resembles breadcrumbs **(4)**. Add enough of the water **(5)** to bring the pastry together, and stir in **(6)**.

Tip onto a lightly floured surface **(7)** and knead lightly to bring the dough together **(8)**. Shape into a flattened ball, wrap in clingfilm/plastic wrap and chill for at least 30 minutes before rolling out and using in the recipe.

The Food Processor Method

Sift the flour and salt together into the bowl of the machine. Add the lard and butter **(9)** and process for about 30 seconds until the mixture resembles fine breadcrumbs **(10)**. Pour in 2 tablespoons of the water **(11)** and pulse for 10 seconds. The dough should start to come together in large raggy lumps **(12)**. If not, add another tablespoon of water and pulse again. As soon as the dough forms one big lump (don't overprocess or the pastry will be tough), tip out onto a lightly floured surface and knead lightly. Shape into a flattened ball, wrap in clingfilm/plastic wrap and chill for at least 30 minutes before rolling out and using in the recipe.

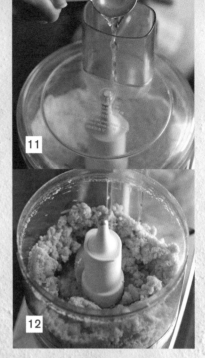

rich shortcrust pastry

This is a wonderfully light and crumbly pastry, but enriched with egg and made with butter only. It is best for richer pies and tarts, or where the taste of the pastry is very important.

250 g/2 cups plain/all-purpose flour

½ teaspoon salt

125 g/1 stick unsalted butter, chilled and diced

2 egg yolks

2–3 tablespoons ice-cold water

Makes about 400 g/14 oz. (enough to line the base of a 23–25-cm/9–10-inch fluted tart pan or to make a double crust for a 20–23-cm/8–9-inch pie plate)

The Classic Way

Sift the flour and salt together into a large mixing bowl and rub in the butter **(1)**.

Mix the egg yolks with the water and add to the bowl **(2)**, stirring to bind to a firm but malleable dough **(3)**.

On a lightly floured surface, knead lightly until smooth, then shape into a flattened ball **(4)**. Wrap in clingfilm/plastic wrap and chill for at least 30 minutes before rolling out and using in the recipe.

The Food Processor Method

Sift the flour and salt together into the bowl of the machine.

Add the butter and process for about 30 seconds until the mixture resembles very fine breadcrumbs. Mix the egg yolks with 2 tablespoons of the water, pour into the food processor and pulse for 10 seconds. The dough should start to come together in large raggy lumps. If not, add another tablespoon of water and pulse again.

As soon as the dough forms one big lump (don't overprocess or the pastry will be tough), tip out onto a lightly floured surface and knead lightly. Shape into a flattened ball, wrap in clingfilm/plastic wrap and chill for at least 30 minutes before rolling out and using in the recipe.

rough puff pastry

This is the quick way to make puff pastry. Rolling and folding the pastry dough creates layers of pastry and pockets of butter. The cooked pastry will be buttery, puffy and light if made well.

250 g/2 cups plain/all-purpose flour

a pinch of salt

150 g/10 tablespoons unsalted butter, chilled

about 150 ml/⅔ cup ice-cold water

Makes about 550 g/1¼ lbs. (enough to line or make a 30-cm/12-inch pie plate or base)

Method

Sift the flour and salt together into a large mixing bowl.

Quickly cut the butter into small cubes, about the size of the top of your little finger.

Stir the butter into the flour with a round-bladed knife so that it is evenly distributed.

Drizzle the water over the surface, then mix with the knife until the dough starts to come together in a messy lump.

Tip out onto a lightly floured surface and knead lightly until it forms a streaky, rather lumpy ball. Flatten the ball with the palm of your hand and wrap in clingfilm/plastic wrap. Chill for 30 minutes until firm.

Unwrap the chilled pastry and, on a lightly floured surface, roll out away from you into a long rectangle, three times longer than it is wide (no exact measurements needed here, but it should be about 1 cm/½ inch thick) **(1)**. Mark the pastry lightly into 3 equal sections with a blunt knife. Now fold the third closest to you up over the middle third. Brush off any excess flour with a dry pastry brush **(2)**, then bring the top third over towards you to cover the folded two thirds **(3)**.

Give the pastry a quarter turn anti-clockwise so that it looks like a closed book. Seal the edges lightly with a rolling pin to stop them sliding out of shape **(4)**. Now roll out, always away from you in one direction, until it is the same-sized rectangle as before. Fold in the bottom and top thirds in the same way as before, wrap in clingfilm/plastic wrap and chill for 15 minutes. Do this rolling and folding four more times, then the pastry is ready to use in the recipe.

american pie crust

To give the crust a richer flavour and golden colour, unsalted butter can be substituted for the cooking fat, or use half butter and half cooking fat.

375 g/3 cups plain/all-purpose flour

a good pinch of salt

250 g/1 cup plus 2 tablespoons white cooking fat/shortening, chilled and diced

1 egg, beaten

1 tablespoon white wine vinegar

4 tablespoons ice-cold water

Makes about 700 g/1 lb. 9 oz. (enough to line the base of two 23-cm/9-inch pie plates or make a 23-cm/9-inch double-crust pie)

Method

Sift the flour and salt into a large mixing bowl and cut in the fat with two round-bladed knives **(1)** until thoroughly combined **(2)**. (You can also do this in a food processor.)

In a separate bowl, mix together the beaten egg, vinegar and water. Pour this wet mixture into the dry mixture **(3)** and cut it in with the knives again **(4)**.

Tip out onto a lightly floured surface and knead lightly until smooth (or knead it in the bowl), then shape into a flattened ball. Wrap in clingfilm/plastic wrap and chill for at least 30 minutes before rolling out and using in the recipe.

TIP: The uncooked dough can be frozen in flattened balls, ready to thaw and roll out as required.

pâte sucrée

French for 'sweet dough', this is a crisp, sweet pastry ideal for fruit tarts or pies. It is easy to make and freezes well.

320 g/2 sticks plus 5 tablespoons salted butter, chilled and cubed

160 g/¾ cup caster/granulated sugar

500 g/4 cups plain/all-purpose flour

1 egg

Makes about 1 kg/2 lbs.

Method

Put the butter, sugar and flour in a large bowl and rub between your fingertips until the texture resembles fine breadcrumbs. (You can add orange or lemon zest at this point if desired.) Add the egg and work the mixture with your hands to a smooth paste.

Wrap the dough in clingfilm/plastic wrap and refrigerate for about 30 minutes until firm.

pâte sablée

This rich, buttery pastry has a crumbly texture that is a little bit difficult to work with, but has such a wonderful, melt-in-the-mouth texture that is worth the extra effort.

200 g/1½ cups plus 2 tablespoons plain/all-purpose flour

50 g/⅓ cup ground almonds

75 g/⅓ cup caster/granulated sugar

160 g/11 tablespoons salted butter, at room temperature, cubed

1 egg yolk

Makes about 500 g/1 lb.

Method

Put the flour, ground almonds and sugar in a large bowl and stir until evenly mixed. Add the butter and use your fingertips to rub it into the mixture until the texture resembles breadcrumbs. Add the egg yolk and, still using your hands, mix and knead until the dough binds together into a tight, smooth ball – it can seem like it will never bind, but have patience, it will!

Wrap the dough in clingfilm/plastic wrap and refrigerate for about 30 minutes until firm. Before use, remove from the refrigerator and allow to stand at room temperature for 10–15 minutes.

There's nothing better than a hot, filling savoury pie. Discover this easy-to-make selection of hearty pies to keep you warm on a winter's day, as well as some lighter summer-inspired options.

savoury pies

50 g/2 oz. dried wild mushrooms

6 tablespoons olive oil or dripping

1 onion, finely chopped

3 garlic cloves, chopped

1 large carrot, finely chopped

2 celery stalks, finely chopped

125 g/4 oz. cubed pancetta or bacon

8 juniper berries, crushed

3 bay leaves

2 tablespoons chopped fresh thyme

2 tablespoons plain/all-purpose flour

1 kg/2 lbs. stewing beef, trimmed and cut into large cubes

300 ml/1¼ cups red wine

2 tablespoons redcurrant or cranberry jelly

600 g ready-rolled puff pastry/ 1 package (17.3 oz.) puff pastry sheets

1 egg, beaten

sea salt and freshly ground black pepper

6 individual pie dishes or 1 large pie dish

Serves 6

steak and wild mushroom pies

This glorious recipe can be made as a large pie, or as individual pies for a special occasion. It can be completely made ahead of time – and even frozen.

Put the mushrooms in a bowl, just cover with hot water and let soak for 30 minutes. Meanwhile, heat half the oil in a large casserole dish, add the onion, garlic, carrot and celery and cook for 5–10 minutes until softening. Stir in the pancetta or bacon and fry with the vegetables until just beginning to brown. Add the juniper berries, bay leaves and thyme, sprinkle in the flour, mix well and set aside.

Heat the remaining olive oil in a large frying pan/skillet and fry the beef quickly (in batches) on all sides until crusty and brown. Transfer to the casserole as you go. When done, deglaze the frying pan/skillet with the wine, let bubble, then scrape up the sediment from the bottom. Pour over the meat and vegetables.

Drain the mushrooms and add to the casserole with 150 ml/⅔ cup of the soaking water and the redcurrant or cranberry jelly. Season very well with salt and pepper, then stir well. Bring to the boil on top of the stove, then simmer for 1½ hours until tender. Let cool overnight.

Next day, spoon the stew into 6 individual pie dishes. Cut out 6 circles of pastry, a good 3 cm/1 inch wider than the dishes. Or, use a large pie dish and roll the pastry wider than the dish, as before. Brush the edges of the dishes with beaten egg. Sit the pastry on top of the rim and press over the edge to seal tightly. Brush with more beaten egg, but don't pierce the tops (the steam must be trapped inside). Set the pies on 2 baking sheets and chill for 30 minutes or until ready to bake. Bake at 220°C (425°F) Gas 7 for 20–25 minutes (or 45 minutes to 1 hour for the large pie) until the pastry is risen, crisp and golden brown. Serve hot.

500 g/1 lb. chuck steak, cut into bite-sized pieces

3 tablespoons plain/all-purpose flour

3 tablespoons butter

2 onions, chopped

2 tablespoons olive oil

250 ml/1 cup beer

500 ml/2 cups beef stock

2 tablespoons Worcestershire sauce

1 tablespoon light soy sauce

350-g pack ready-made shortcrust pastry/12-oz. package ready-made pie crust dough, thawed if frozen

1 egg yolk, beaten with 1 tablespoon water

a ceramic pie dish

Serves 4

beef pie

All you need to go with with this iconic Australian recipe is a good helping of mash and peas.

Put the beef in a colander. Sprinkle with the flour and use your hands to toss the pieces until they are coated in flour – let any excess flour fall through the colander.

Heat the butter in a large, heavy-based saucepan set over medium/high heat. Add the onions and cook for 5 minutes, until golden. Remove from the pan and set aside.

Add 1 tablespoon of the oil to the pan. Add half of the beef and cook for about 4–5 minutes, until browned all over. Remove from the pan and set aside. Add the remaining oil to the pan and repeat with the remaining beef. Remove from the pan.

Add the beer, stock and sauces to the pan and bring to the boil. Return the beef to the pan, cook briefly, then reduce the heat to low. Cover and cook for 1 hour, stirring occasionally. Add the onions and increase the heat to high. Boil for about 15–20 minutes, until the gravy is thick and dark. Let cool completely.

Preheat the oven to 200°C (400°F) Gas 6 and put a baking sheet on the centre shelf of the oven.

Lightly flour a work surface. Roll the pastry out to a thickness of about 5 mm/¼ inch. Use a sharp knife to cut a circle slightly larger than the top of the pie dish. Re-roll the remaining pastry and use a knife to cut long strips about 1½ cm/½ inch wide. Brush some of the egg wash around the rim of the pie dish and press the pastry strips around the edge. Brush the pastry with egg wash and put the pastry lid on top. Use a fork to press down around the edge to seal and brush all over the remaining egg wash. Bake in the preheated oven for about 45–50 minutes, until the pastry is golden and crisp.

steak and kidney pie

For the pastry:

175 g/1½ sticks salted butter, chilled and cubed

350 g/2¾ cups self-raising/ rising flour

salt, to taste

200 ml/¾ cup cold whole milk, plus extra to glaze

For the filling:

4 lamb's kidneys

750 g/1 lb. 10 oz. stewing beef, diced

250 g/9 oz. dark open-cup mushrooms

1 large onion, finely chopped

4–6 tablespoons chopped fresh parsley

1 tablespoon chopped fresh thyme

½ teaspoon crumbled bay leaves

1–2 tablespoons plain/ all-purpose flour

600 ml/2½ cups dark beef stock

1 tablespoon English mustard powder

sea salt and freshly ground black pepper

a 1.5-litre/quart oval pie dish

a pie funnel

Serves 6

This British classic is so easy to make, as the meat requires no browning. Adding really dark stock gives it a lovely colour.

Preheat the oven to 170°C (325°F) Gas 3.

For the filling, prepare the kidneys by splitting them in half and snipping out and discarding the creamy core. Slice or roughly chop the kidneys and add them to a large mixing bowl with the diced beef, mushrooms, onion, herbs, flour and plenty of salt and pepper.

In a separate bowl, combine the beef stock and mustard powder, stirring until the powder has dissolved, then pour into the mixing bowl with the other ingredients. Stir thoroughly and then pile the filling into the pie dish, pushing the pie funnel into the centre – it should fill the dish generously.

Now make the pastry. Put the butter, flour and salt into a large mixing bowl and use a round-bladed knife to chop and cut the butter into the flour until it resembles rough breadcrumbs. Stir in the milk and mix to a soft dough.

Tip the dough out onto a lightly floured surface and roll out to an oval shape that is slightly larger than the top of the dish. Cut off an extra long strip of pastry that will fit around the lip of the pie dish. Brush the lip of the pie dish with milk and press the pastry strip around the lip. Brush this with milk and lay the pastry oval over the dish, letting it fall on top of the pie funnel in the centre. Cut a cross in the pastry touching the pie funnel and gently push it over the funnel. Press the pastry onto the lip of the dish to seal and trim off the excess pastry. Crimp the pastry together and then brush the top of the pie with milk.

Stand the pie dish in a baking pan and bake in the preheated oven for 1¾ hours until golden and bubbling.

shepherd's pie

2 tablespoons olive oil

125 g/1 stick butter

2 large onions, chopped

2 carrots, grated

2 celery sticks, chopped

750 g/1½ lbs. minced/ground lamb

1 litre/quart beef stock

2½ tablespoons cornflour/cornstarch

a large handful of flat-leaf parsley leaves, finely chopped

1 kg/2¼ lbs. baking potatoes, peeled and quartered or halved, depending on size

85 ml/⅓ cup milk

sea salt and freshly ground black pepper

a large ovenproof baking dish

Serves 6

If you want it your shepherd's pie a little smarter, bake it in individual ovenproof dishes.

Heat the oil and 1 tablespoon of the butter in large, heavy-based frying pan/skillet set over high heat. When the butter has melted and is sizzling, add the onions and cook for 5 minutes, until golden. Add the carrots and celery and cook for a further 5 minutes. Add the minced/ground lamb and cook for 10 minutes, until it has browned, stirring often to break up any large clumps.

Put the cornflour/cornstarch in a small bowl and stir in 65 ml/¼ cup of the stock. Add the remaining stock to the pan with the lamb and cook for 10 minutes, letting the stock boil and reduce a little. Add the cornflour/cornstarch mixture to the pan and cook, stirring constantly, until the liquid thickens to a gravy. Stir in the parsley, season well with salt and pepper and set aside.

Preheat the oven to 180°C (350°F) Gas 4.

Put the potatoes in a large saucepan of lightly salted boiling water. Cook for 10 minutes, until they are just starting to break up and the water is cloudy. Drain well and return to the warm pan. Add the remaining butter and the milk and season to taste with salt and pepper. Roughly mash to leave the potatoes with a chunky texture.

Spoon the lamb into the baking dish and spread the mashed potatoes over the top. Cook in the preheated oven for about 40–45 minutes, until the potato is crisp and golden brown.

1 tablespoon vegetable oil

1 onion, finely chopped

1 green (bell) pepper, finely chopped

500 g/1 lb. minced/ground pork or beef

2 teaspoons chilli powder

1 teaspoon ground cumin

½ teaspoon cayenne pepper

½ teaspoon allspice

400-g/14-oz. can kidney beans or black beans, drained

400-g/14-oz. can chopped tomatoes

100 g/½ cup stoned/pitted black olives, sliced

150 g/1 cup sweetcorn/corn kernels

1 tablespoon Worcestershire sauce

Tabasco sauce (optional)

For the topping:

300 g/1 cup plain/all-purpose flour

300 g/1 cup cornmeal

2 teaspoons baking powder

¼ teaspoon salt

a pinch of sugar

3 tablespoons melted butter

180 ml/¾ cup milk or buttermilk

1 egg, beaten

1 small fresh green chilli/chile, very finely chopped

45 g/½ cup mild Cheddar, grated

a 30 x 20 cm/12 x baking dish

Serves 4–6

tamale pie

This pie is topped with a golden cornbread topping, instead of the traditional masa harina, which is not always easy to obtain. It's easy to prepare and is a great recipe to experiment with. You can always use leftover roast meat instead of minced/ground pork next time.

Preheat the oven to 190°C (375°F) Gas 5.

Heat the oil in a frying pan/skillet. Add the onion and green (bell) pepper and cook for about 5 minutes, until soft. Season and add the minced/ground pork or beef, chilli powder, cumin, cayenne and allspice. Cook, stirring often, until browned.

Stir in the beans, tomatoes, olives, sweetcorn/corn kernels and Worcestershire sauce. Reduce the heat and simmer, uncovered, for about 10–15 minutes.

Meanwhile, prepare the topping. Put the flour, cornmeal, baking powder, salt and sugar in a bowl and stir to combine. Stir in the melted butter, milk and egg and stir just until blended. Stir in the chilli/chile and cheese. Add an extra spoonful of milk if the mixture seems dry.

Taste the pork or beef mixture and adjust the seasoning if necessary. Add some Tabasco if it is not hot enough. Spoon into the baking dish and spread evenly. Drop the cornmeal mixture in spoonfuls on top, spreading evenly to cover.

Bake in the preheated oven for about 30 minutes, until the topping is golden brown. Serve immediately.

Variation: For a vegetarian version, replace the minced/ground pork or beef with an additional can of beans and add 1–2 diced courgettes/zucchini, cooked along with the onion and pepper.

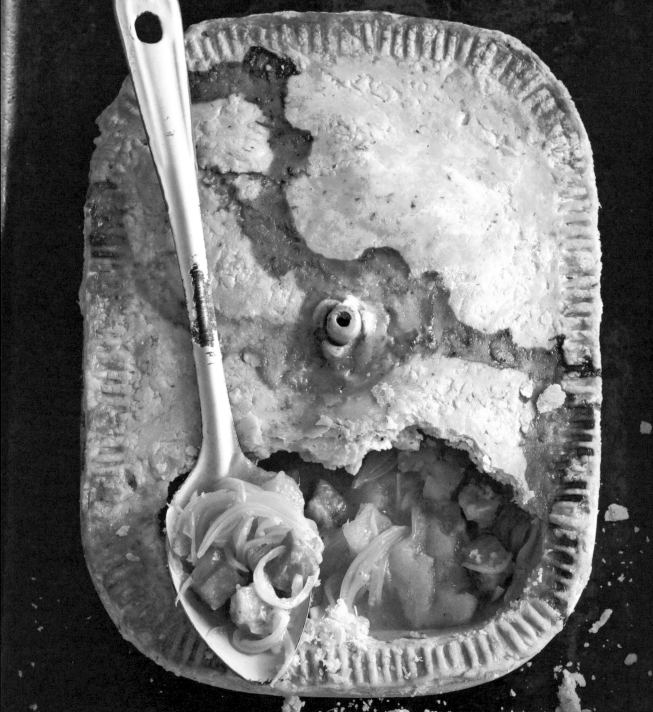

For the suet crust pastry:

225 g/1¾ cups plain/all-purpose flour

½ teaspoon salt

50 g/2½ tablespoons lard

50 g/4 tablespoons shredded beef or vegetable suet

1 teaspoon dried mixed herbs

2–3 tablespoons ice-cold water

3–4 tablespoons milk, to glaze

For the filling:

450 g/1 lb. cooked ham, diced

3 tablespoons plain/all-purpose flour, seasoned with salt and black pepper

2 tablespoons soft light brown sugar

¼ teaspoon freshly grated nutmeg

¼ teaspoon ground allspice

450 g/1 lb. cooking apples, peeled, cored and quartered

2 onions, thinly sliced

300 ml/1¼ cups dry (hard) cider

sea salt and freshly ground black pepper

a 900-ml/1-quart pie dish

a pie funnel

Serves 4–6

ham and apple pie

Serve this with a robust vegetable such as broccoli, cabbage or sprouts and boiled, buttered new potatoes. Cook in deep individual dishes if you have the time.

Preheat the oven to 200°C (400°F) Gas 6.

To make the pastry, sift the flour and salt into a large mixing bowl, add the lard and rub in with your fingertips until combined. Stir in the suet and herbs and mix to a soft dough with just enough of the water to bind. Knead lightly until smooth, then leave to rest in a cool place until required.

Toss the diced ham in the seasoned flour to lightly coat. Mix the sugar and spices together in a separate bowl.

Put half the ham in the pie dish and cover with half the apples, then half the spice mixture and half the onion slices. Repeat these layers, seasoning between each one, then pour in the cider.

On a lightly floured surface, roll out the pastry and make a small slit in the centre to fit over the pie funnel. Dampen the edges of the pie dish with a little milk and cover with the pastry. Brush the pastry with milk, set the pie dish on a baking sheet and bake in the preheated oven for 20 minutes. Reduce the temperature to 180°C (350°F) Gas 4 and bake for a further hour until golden (covering the top with kitchen foil if you feel the pastry is becoming too dark).

1 small rotisserie chicken

3 tablespoons butter

1 leek, sliced

1 carrot, diced

1 celery stick, diced

125 ml/½ cup dry white wine

3 tablespoons plain/all-purpose flour

500 ml/2 cups chicken stock

100 g/¾ cup frozen peas

125 ml/½ cup single/light cream

1 sheet ready-rolled puff pastry, thawed if frozen

1 egg yolk, beaten with 1 tablespoon water

sea salt and freshly ground black pepper

4 baking dishes, each about 250 ml/1 cup capacity

Serves 4

chicken pot pie

The filling for these comforting pies is made with ready-cooked rotisserie chicken. The meat can be shredded and used warm or cold in salads or diced and added to soups, stir-fries and pasta sauces.

Preheat the oven to 180°C (350°F) Gas 4.

Remove the skin from the chicken, slice the meat off the bones and chop finely. Set aside until needed.

Melt the butter in a large saucepan set over high heat and add the leek, carrot and celery. Sauté for 5 minutes, until softened. Add the wine and cook for a further 5 minutes, until it has almost evaporated. Add the chicken and stir well to combine. Sprinkle the flour into the pan. Cook for 1 minute, then gradually pour in the stock, stirring constantly as you do so. Bring to the boil and cook uncovered, stirring often, for 2–3 minutes, until the mixture has thickened. Add the peas and cream to the pan and stir well. Cook for 1 minute, then remove from the heat. Season to taste with salt and pepper and let cool to room temperature.

Spoon the mixture into the baking dishes. Unroll the pastry and lay it on a lightly floured work surface. Use a sharp knife to cut circles from the pastry just slightly larger than the top of the dishes. Put a pastry circle on top of each dish, folding the pastry over the side and pressing down firmly with the tines of a fork. Brush with the egg wash and cook in the preheated oven for about 25–30 minutes, until the pastry is puffed and golden.

4 skinless, boneless
chicken thighs

2 large skinless, boneless
chicken breasts

100 g/3½ oz. bacon lardons
(or 3 slices of lean slab bacon,
sliced into short strips)

1 onion, thinly sliced

100 g/3½ oz. chestnut/cremini
mushrooms, quartered or
thickly sliced

3 tablespoons chopped fresh
flat-leaf parsley

2 teaspoons mushroom
ketchup, Worcestershire sauce
or soy sauce

4 tablespoons chicken stock

½ quantity Basic Shortcrust Pastry
(see pages 12–13)

1 egg, beaten with a pinch of salt,
to glaze

sea salt and freshly ground
black pepper

a 900-ml/1-quart, deep pie dish

a pie funnel

Serves 4–6

chicken and mushroom pie

Simple to make and one of the very best everyday pies, this dish is made all the more delicious by the addition of mushroom ketchup, a deeply-flavoured seasoning sauce.

Preheat the oven to 190°C (375°F) Gas 5 and place the pie funnel in the centre of the dish.

Cut the chicken into large pieces and mix with the bacon lardons/strips. Layer the chicken mixture into the pie dish with the onion, mushrooms, parsley, salt and pepper. Mix the mushroom ketchup (or alternative) with the chicken stock and pour over the filling.

Roll out the pastry on a lightly floured surface, making sure it is not too thin. Make a small hole in the centre of the pastry to fit over the pie funnel and use it to cover the pie. Crimp, scallop or fork the edges to seal. Brush with beaten egg and bake in the preheated oven for 1½ hours until golden.

350 g/12 oz. raw shell-on tiger prawns/shrimp

700 ml/3 cups milk

1 onion, chopped

1 bay leaf

2 peppercorns

450 g/1 lb. fresh sustainable white fish fillets (such as cod, haddock pollack), skin on

450 g/1 lb. undyed smoked haddock or cod fillet, skin on

75 g/5 tablespoons butter

75 g/½ cup plus 1 tablespoon plain/all-purpose flour

4 tablespoons chopped fresh flat-leaf parsley

sea salt and freshly ground black pepper

For the saffron and dill mash:

1.3 kg/3 lbs. floury potatoes, peeled

a large pinch of saffron threads soaked in 3 tablespoons hot water

75 g/5 tablespoons butter

250 ml/1 cup milk

3 tablespoons chopped fresh dill

a 1.5-litre/quart oval pie dish

Serves 4–6

glorious golden fish pie

This is a British favourite and is worth spending the time to get it right. The secret of a moist and juicy fish pie is not to overcook the fish and not to pre-cook the prawns/shrimp.

Peel the shells from the prawns/shrimp. Put the shells in a saucepan with the milk, onion, bay leaf and peppercorns. Bring to the boil then lower the heat and simmer for 10 minutes. Turn off the heat and set aside to infuse.

Lay the white and smoked fish fillets, skin side up, in a roasting pan. Strain the infused milk into the pan and and simmer on the hob/stovetop for 5–7 minutes until just opaque. Lift the fish fillets out of the milk and transfer to a plate. When the fillets are cool enough to handle, pull off the skin and flake the fish into large pieces, removing any bones as you go. Transfer to a large bowl and add the shelled prawns/shrimp.

Melt the butter in a small saucepan set over medium heat, stir in the flour and gradually add the flavoured milk from the roasting pan. Whisk well and simmer gently for 15 minutes until thick and a little reduced. Taste and season with salt and pepper. Stir in the parsley and pour the sauce over the fish. Carefully mix everything together, then transfer the mixture to the pie dish and leave to cool.

Preheat the oven to 180°C (350°F) Gas 4.

Boil the potatoes in salted water until soft, drain well and mash. Beat in the saffron and its soaking water (if using), butter, milk and dill. When the fish mixture is cold, spoon over the golden mash, piling it up gloriously on top. Bake in the preheated oven for 30–40 minutes or until the potato is golden brown and crispy. If it fails to brown enough, finish it off under a medium grill/broiler. Serve immediately!

snapper pie

This fish pie is very different to the béchamel sauce recipes you may have cooked before. The delicious sweet onion sauce is based on the French classic 'soubise'. Be ready to give the recipe to your guests!

1 tablespoon olive oil

1 tablespoon butter

900 g/2 lbs. white onions, thinly sliced

2 fresh or dry bay leaves

375 ml/1½ cups fish stock

500 ml/2 cups single/light cream

1 sheet ready-rolled puff pastry, thawed if frozen

800 g/1½ lbs. red snapper fillet, cut into bite-sized pieces

milk, for glazing

sea salt and freshly ground black pepper

4 individual ovenproof baking dishes, about 10–15 cm/4–6 inch diameter

Serves 4

Heat the olive oil and butter in a heavy-based saucepan set over medium heat. Add the onions and bay leaves and stir well to break up the onions. Cover and cook for about 30 minutes, stirring often so that the onions sweat and soften. Remove the lid and increase the heat to high. Cook for a further 10 minutes, stirring occasionally so that the onions do not catch and are a pale caramel colour.

Add the fish stock, bring to the boil and cook until the liquid has reduced by half. Reduce the heat to medium and add the cream. Cook for about 15 minutes, stirring constantly. Remove from the heat and let cool. Remove the bay leaves and blend the sauce in a food processor until smooth. Set aside until needed.

Preheat the oven to 220°C (425°F) Gas 7.

Lightly flour a work surface. Roll the pastry out to a thickness of about 2–3 mm/⅛ inch. Cut 4 circles from the pastry, using an upturned baking dish as a template.

Spoon half of the onion sauce into each of the baking dishes. Arrange a quarter of the fish pieces on top, then spoon over the remaining sauce. Repeat to fill 4 pies. Cover each pie with a pastry circle and press around the edges with the tines of a fork to seal. Use a sharp knife to make 2–3 small incisions in the pastry to let the steam escape. Brush the top of each with a little milk to glaze and bake in the preheated oven for 20–25 minutes, until golden and puffed. Serve with a watercress salad, if liked.

mashed potato pie with bacon, leeks and cheese

If you've got a successful crop of potatoes this year and you need inspiration for how best to use them, this pie is a great option. Bacon, leeks and cheese make a particularly perfect trio, but you can add just about anything to this versatile dish.

1 kg/2¼ lbs. floury potatoes, peeled

2 tablespoons olive oil

1 onion, finely chopped

2 small leeks, thinly sliced

90 g/3½ oz thick-sliced bacon or pancetta, diced

2 tablespoons butter

250 ml/1 cup milk or single/light cream (or a bit of both)

1 egg, beaten

a pinch of paprika

a large handful of fresh flat-leaf parsley leaves, chopped

90 g/⅔ cup grated firm cheese, such as Gruyère

sea salt and freshly ground black pepper

a 24-cm/10-inch round baking dish, well buttered

Serves 4–6

Halve or quarter the potatoes depending on their size; they should be about the same to cook evenly. Put them in a large saucepan, add sufficient cold water to cover, salt well and bring to the boil. Simmer for about 20 minutes, until tender.

Meanwhile, heat the oil in a frying pan/skillet set over low heat. Add the onion and leeks and cook gently for about 10 minutes, until soft. Add the bacon or pancetta and cook for 3–5 minutes, until just browned. Season with salt and set aside.

Preheat the oven to 190°C (375°F) Gas 5.

Drain the potatoes and mash coarsely, mixing in the butter and milk. Season well and add the egg. Stir to combine thoroughly.

Stir in the leek mixture, paprika, parsley and half the cheese. Transfer to the prepared baking dish and spread evenly. Sprinkle over the remaining cheese and bake in the preheated oven for 35–45 minutes, until well browned. Serve immediately.

2 tablespoons Greek olive oil

1 bunch of spring onions/scallions, finely sliced

2 garlic cloves, crushed

450 g/1 lb. young spinach leaves, washed

4 large eggs, beaten

200 g/7 oz. feta cheese, crumbled

1 teaspoon freeze-dried oregano

a large pinch of freshly grated nutmeg

finely grated zest of 1 lemon

4 large sheets of thin Greek-style filo/phyllo pastry (about 225 g/8 oz.)

75 g/5 tablespoons butter, melted

sea salt and freshly ground black pepper

a 25 x 20-cm/10 x 8-inch baking pan

Serves 6

greek spinach, feta and oregano filo pie

This light and flavoursome Greek pie works well with ricotta or even English Wensleydale if you aren't partial to salty feta.

Preheat the oven to 190°C (375°F) Gas Mark 5.

Heat the oil in a large saucepan, add the spring onions/scallions and garlic and sauté for 2 minutes. Pile in the spinach, cover with a lid and cook for 3 minutes over a high heat or until the leaves are just wilted. Tip into a sieve/strainer and press out the excess moisture. Transfer to a large mixing bowl and stir in the eggs, feta, oregano, nutmeg, lemon zest, a little salt and plenty of pepper, mixing well.

Brush the inside of the baking pan with melted butter. Carefully brush the filo/phyllo pastry sheets all over with melted butter.

Lay the first sheet of pastry in the pan, pressing it into the base and up the sides. Place the second sheet on top at 90 degrees, making sure the pastry will overhang the pan. Repeat with the remaining 2 sheets of pastry.

Spoon the filling into the pastry-lined pan and level. Fold over the overlapping pastry, brushing with more butter as necessary. Brush the top with the remaining butter.

Bake in the preheated oven for 50–60 minutes until the pastry is golden brown and crisp. Remove from the oven and cover with a clean dish towel for 5 minutes to lightly soften the pastry before you mark it. With a sharp knife, mark the pie into 6 squares and leave to cool. Serve warm or cold.

TIP: For a neater look to the top of the pie, use only 3½ sheets of pastry to line the pan, saving a half sheet to lay over the top and neaten the look. Brush with butter before baking.

swiss chard, feta and egg pie

The pastry used for this delicious pie is based on the Turkish version of pizza dough (pide).

3 tablespoons olive oil

2 garlic cloves, sliced

1 red onion, sliced

500 g/1 lb. Swiss chard, cut into 2-cm/¾ inch pieces

4 eggs

200 g/7 oz. feta cheese, crumbled

sea salt and freshly ground black pepper

For the pastry:

250 g/2 cups plain/all-purpose flour

150 g/1 stick plus 2 tablespoons unsalted butter, cubed

2 egg yolks

2–3 tablespoons iced water

Serves 6

To make the pastry, put the flour and butter in the bowl of a food processor and put the bowl in the freezer for 10 minutes. Pulse the ingredients a few times until just combined. With the motor of the food processor running, add the egg yolks and just enough iced water so that the mixture is on the verge of coming together. Do not overbeat, as this will make the pastry tough. Remove the dough from the bowl and use lightly floured hands to quickly form it into a ball. Wrap in clingfilm/plastic wrap and let rest in the fridge for 30 minutes.

Put 2 tablespoons of the oil in a frying pan/skillet set over high heat, add the onion and garlic and cook for 2 minutes, until it softens. Add the Swiss chard to the pan and cook for about 5 minutes, stirring often, until it wilts and softens. Season well with salt and pepper, leave in the pan and set aside to cool.

Preheat the oven to 220°C (425°F) Gas 7.

Roll the pastry dough out on a sheet of lightly floured parchment paper to form a circle about 35 cm/14 inches in diameter, trimming away any uneven bits. Roll the edge over to form a 1-cm/½-inch border, then roll over again. Transfer the pastry circle to a baking sheet. Spoon the Swiss chard mixture over the pastry. Put the eggs in a bowl and prick the yolks with a fork. Pour the eggs over the Swiss chard so that they are evenly distributed, then scatter the feta over the top. Drizzle the remaining oil over the pie and cook in the preheated oven for about 20 minutes, until the pastry is golden and the top of the pie is just starting to turn brown. Let cool for 10 minutes before cutting into slices to serve.

Discover a whole new world of pleasure, including a gorgeous Lattice-topped Cherry Pie, a delightful Rhubarb Meringue Pie and American classics like Key Lime Pie, Shoofly Pie and Mississippi Mud Pie.

sweet pies

deep-dish caramel apple pie

Noone can resist a homemade apple pie! This version adds smashed-up toffees/caramels to the apples that melt into the pie while it cooks, cloaking the apples in caramel.

75 g/3 oz. hard toffees/caramels

1 kg/2¼ lbs. dessert apples (such as Cox's, Russet, McIntosh or Macoun), peeled, cored and thickly sliced

finely grated zest and freshly squeezed juice of 1 small lemon

3 cloves

½ teaspoon mixed/apple pie spice (or cinnamon if you prefer)

1 quantity Basic Shortcrust Pastry (see pages 12–13)

1 tablespoon each plain/all-purpose flour and caster/granulated sugar, mixed, plus extra caster/granulated sugar for dredging

1 small egg white

a 23-cm/9-inch pie plate

Serves 6

Preheat the oven to 200°C (400°F) Gas 6.

Put the toffees in a plastic bag and use a rolling pin to smash them into small pieces. Add them to a large mixing bowl with the apples, lemon juice and zest, cloves and mixed spice/apple pie spice.

Divide the pastry into 2 pieces and, on a lightly floured surface, roll out each piece to a circle that will easily cover the pie plate. Line the plate with one of the pastry circles and sprinkle the base with the flour and sugar mix. Spoon the apple mixture into the pie plate and mound up in the centre. Brush the pastry edges with a little water and cover the pie dish with the remaining pastry circle, sealing and crimping the edges. Cut off any excess pastry and use the trimmings to cut shapes to decorate the pie, if you have time. Make a slit through the pastry on top to allow the steam to escape while cooking.

Beat the egg white to a loose froth and brush evenly all over the pie, then dredge generously with sugar. Set the pie on a baking sheet and bake in the preheated oven for about 35–40 minutes until golden and firm with a sugary crust.

moroccan apple pie

The method of using layers of buttered filo/phyllo pastry and inverting the pie was inspired by Moroccan 'bastilla'.

6 tart green apples, peeled, cored and thinly sliced

1 teaspoon finely grated lemon zest

2 tablespoons freshly squeezed lemon juice

1 vanilla pod/bean

115 g/½ cup plus 2 tablespoons caster/superfine sugar

1 teaspoon ground cinnamon

1 teaspoon cornflour/cornstarch

80 g/6 tablespoons unsalted butter, melted and cooled

8 sheets of filo/phyllo pastry, thawed if frozen

icing/confectioners' sugar, for dusting

a loose-based cake pan, 22-cm/9-inches diameter, lined with parchment paper

Serves 8–10

Put the apples in a non-reactive bowl with the lemon zest and juice. Rub the vanilla pod/bean between your palms to soften it, then use a sharp knife to split it open lengthways. Scrape the seeds into the bowl with the apples. Add half of the caster/superfine sugar and toss to coat. Put the remaining caster/superfine sugar in a small bowl with the cinnamon and mix to combine. Set aside.

Put the apples in a saucepan with 2 tablespoons water and set over medium heat. Cover and cook for 10 minutes, stirring occasionally, until the apples are soft but not mushy. Transfer the apples to a bowl and let cool. When completely cool, stir in the cornflour/cornstarch.

Preheat the oven to 220°C (425°F) Gas 7. Put a baking sheet in the oven to heat. Brush the cake pan with a little of the melted butter.

Lay a sheet of filo/phyllo on a clean work surface and lightly brush with melted butter. Sprinkle over some of the cinnamon sugar. Repeat using 3 more sheets of filo/phyllo. Lift the filo/phyllo into the cake pan. Gently press it into the pan letting the ends hang over the rim. Repeat with the remaining filo/phyllo, but lay the second stack across the first one so that the entire rim of the pan is draped in pastry. Spoon the apples into the pan and use the back of a spoon to gently press them down. Fold the ends of the filo/phyllo towards the centre of the pan to enclose the filling. Lightly brush with melted butter.

Remove the baking sheet from the oven and line with parchment paper. Carefully invert the pan onto the baking sheet. Remove the side and base of the pan and brush the top of the pie with melted butter. Bake in the preheated oven for 30–35 minutes, until golden. Dust liberally with icing/confectioners' sugar and serve warm.

For the American cream cheese pastry:

300 g/2⅓ cups plain/all-purpose flour

2 tablespoons icing/confectioners' sugar

a large pinch of salt

175 g/½ sticks unsalted butter, chilled and diced

175 g/¾ cup Philadelphia cream cheese

4–6 tablespoons milk, chilled, plus extra to glaze

For the cherry filling:

3 x 350-g/12-oz. packs frozen pitted Morello cherries (or 1 kg/2¼ lbs., drained weight, canned Morello cherries)

200 g/1 cup caster/granulated sugar, plus extra for sprinkling

½ teaspoon ground cinnamon or a good pinch of allspice

freshly squeezed juice of 1 lemon

5 tablespoons cornflour/cornstarch

a 23-cm/9-inch metal or enamel pie plate

a baking sheet lined with non-stick parchment paper

Serves 6

lattice-topped cherry pie

This pie is so simple and is best made with luscious Morello cherries. Serve with cream or vanilla ice cream.

For the pastry, sift the flour into a large mixing bowl with the icing/confectioners' sugar and salt. Rub in the butter and cream cheese until the mixture resembles coarse breadcrumbs. Add enough of the milk to mix to a soft dough. Gather up the dough to form a ball and knead very briefly until smooth. Divide into 2 pieces, then wrap and chill both portions in the fridge for at least 1 hour.

For the filling, mix the cherries with all the remaining ingredients and leave to stand for 20 minutes, then stir once more.

Preheat the oven to 220°C (425°F) Gas 7.

On a lightly floured surface, roll out half the pastry and use it to line the pie plate. Roll out the second half of the dough to a rectangle and cut into wide strips long enough to drape over the pie. Put the strips onto the prepared baking sheet and chill until needed.

Spoon the cherries into the lined pie plate, mounding them up in the centre. Brush the edges of the pastry with water, then lay the pastry strips on top, weaving them to form a lattice. Trim the edges, then crimp to seal. Brush the top with milk and sprinkle with sugar.

Set the pie on a baking sheet to catch any juices and bake in the preheated oven for 20 minutes to set the pastry. Reduce the oven temperature to 180°C (350°F) Gas 4 and bake for a further 30–40 minutes until the thickened cherry juices bubble up through the lattice. Cover the top loosely with kitchen foil if the pastry looks as if it is browning too quickly. Serve warm or cold.

pumpkin pie

If you can't find pumpkin puree, don't worry – butternut squash purée makes an ideal substitute and gives a lovely brightness to the filling.

1 quantity Basic Shortcrust Pastry (see pages 12–13)

475-g/15-oz. can pumpkin purée or 500 ml/2 cups of homemade (see below)

100 g/½ cup packed soft light brown sugar

3 eggs

200 ml/¾ cup evaporated milk or double/heavy cream

120 ml/½ cup golden syrup/light corn syrup or light molasses

a good pinch of salt

1 teaspoon ground cinnamon

½ teaspoon mixed/apple pie spice

1 teaspoon pure vanilla extract

2 tablespoons golden or spiced rum (optional)

a 20.5-cm/8-inch metal or enamel pie plate

a maple leaf pastry cutter (optional)

Serves 4–6

Preheat the oven to 190°C (375°F) Gas 5.

Roll out the pastry thinly on a lightly floured surface and use it to line the pie plate, trimming off the excess pastry. Either crimp the edge of the pastry or use the pastry trimmings to cut leaves to decorate the edge. Prick the base all over with a fork, then line with parchment paper or kitchen foil and baking beans and bake blind (see page 11) for 12–15 minutes. Remove the foil and beans and return to the oven for a further 5 minutes to dry out the pastry. Leave to cool.

Reduce the oven temperature to 160°C (325°F) Gas 3.

Place all the remaining ingredients in a food processor and process until smooth. Set the cooled pie crust on a baking sheet and pour in the filling. Bake in the preheated oven for about 1 hour or until just set. If the pastry edges are beginning to brown too much before the filling is set, cover the edges with kitchen foil before returning to the oven. Remove from the oven to a wire rack and leave to cool in the pie plate. Serve warm or at room temperature, not chilled.

TIP: If you can't find cans of pumpkin or butternut squash purée, you can prepare your own. Cut 750 g/1½ lbs. of unpeeled pumpkin or squash into large chunks and bake in an oven preheated to 160°C (325°F) Gas 3 for about 1 hour. Alternatively, cook the chunks of pumpkin in the microwave in a covered heatproof bowl. (Boiling it won't work as it will make the pumpkin too wet.) When cooled, scrape the flesh from the skin and purée in a food processor.

fresh date and ginger cream pie

Medjool dates give a rich fudgey sweetness to this creamy tart. If you're a real date lover, then double the amount of dates and halve the custard.

½ quantity American Pie Crust (see page 16), made with 1 teaspoon ground ginger sifted with the flour

250 g/9 oz. fresh Medjool dates

2 balls stem ginger in syrup, drained and finely chopped

2 tablespoons brandy (optional)

350 ml/1⅓ cups sour cream

125 g/½ cup plus 1 tablespoon golden caster/natural cane sugar

2 tablespoons cornflour/cornstarch

2.5-cm/1-inch piece fresh ginger, grated

⅛ teaspoon ground ginger

3 large eggs, beaten

2 teaspoons pure vanilla extract

a pinch of sea salt

a 23-cm/9-inch pie plate

Serves 8

Roll out the pastry on a lightly floured surface and use it to line the pie plate. Trim off any excess pastry and use it to cut shapes to decorate the edge of the pie. Prick the base with a fork and and chill for at least 30 minutes.

Preheat the oven to 200°C (400°F) Gas 6 and set a heavy baking sheet on the middle shelf.

Slit each date along its length and flick out the pit. Keep them whole and fill each one with a little of the chopped stem ginger, then sprinkle with the brandy (if using). Arrange the dates over the base of the pie crust, open edge uppermost.

In a large mixing bowl, whisk together the sour cream, sugar, cornflour/cornstarch, fresh and ground gingers, beaten eggs, vanilla and salt. Pour this over the dates, being careful not to dislodge them.

Place the pie on the baking sheet in the preheated oven and bake for 10 minutes. Reduce the oven temperature to 180°C (350°F) Gas 4 and bake for a further 30 minutes or until the centre is set.

Remove the pie to wire rack and leave to cool. Serve slightly warm or cold, just as it is.

1 quantity American Pie Crust
(see page 16)

150 g/1 cup large juicy raisins,
chopped

3 tablespoons spiced rum, warm

2 large eggs

225 g/1 cup plus 2 tablespoons
caster/superfine sugar

250 ml/1 cup sour cream

1 tablespoon freshly squeezed
lemon juice

¼ teaspoon freshly grated nutmeg

a good pinch of salt

2–3 tablespoons demerara
sugar, for dredging

a 23-cm/9-inch metal pie plate

Serves 4–6

sour cream raisin pie

This is almost like a very light cheesecake baked in a double crust – very rich and luscious. Rich shortcrust pastry also works with great success.

Preheat the oven to 230°C (450°F) Gas 8 and set a heavy baking sheet on the middle shelf.

Divide the pastry dough into 2 pieces. Roll one half out on a lightly floured surface and use it to line the pie plate. Trim off the excess pastry.

Soak the chopped raisins in the rum for about an hour until the rum is absorbed.

Using an electric hand whisk, whisk the eggs with the caster/superfine sugar until the mixture is pale and mousse-like. Set aside.

Reserve 2 tablespoons of the sour cream for the glaze. Whip the remaining sour cream with the lemon juice, nutmeg and salt until slightly thickened. Carefully fold into the egg mixture, then fold in the soaked chopped raisins. Spoon into the pie crust.

Roll out the remaining pastry thinly so that it will cover the top of the pie. Brush the edges of the pie with a little water, pick up the pastry on the rolling pin and lift it over the pie to cover it. Fold the top crust carefully under the lower crust and press the edges together to seal. Brush with the reserved sour cream and dredge with the demerara. Slash the top a couple of times to allow the steam to escape. Place the pie on the baking sheet in the preheated oven and bake for 10 minutes. Reduce the oven temperature to 180°C (350°F) Gas 4 and bake for a further 20 minutes until the pastry is set and pale coloured. Leave to cool before serving.

double cranberry and orange pie

The popped cranberries glisten through the lattice top and stain the pastry with bubbling juices.

1 quantity American Pie Crust (see page 16)

300 g/3 cups fresh or unthawed frozen cranberries

100 g/¾ cup dried cranberries

100 g/½ cup caster/superfine sugar, plus extra for dredging

3 tablespoons golden syrup/light corn syrup

finely grated zest and freshly squeezed juice of 1 tangerine

3 tablespoons orange liqueur

30 g/2 tablespoons butter

a little milk, for brushing

a 23-cm/9-inch metal pie plate

a baking sheet lined with non-stick parchment paper

Serves 6–8

Cut the pastry into 2 pieces, one slightly larger than the other. Roll out the larger piece to a circle just larger than the pie plate and the smaller piece to a rectangle measuring about 25 x 8 cm/10 x 3 inches. Use the circle to line the pie plate but do not trim the edges yet. Slip the pastry rectangle onto the prepared baking sheet and cut eight lattice strips about 1 cm/½ inch wide using a sharp knife. Chill both the pie crust and lattice strips in the fridge for 30 minutes.

Preheat oven to 220°C (425°F) Gas 7.

Put the fresh and dried cranberries into a mixing bowl, add the sugar, syrup, tangerine zest and juice and orange liqueur and stir to mix well. Tip the mixture into the chilled pie crust and dot with the butter. Dampen the rim of the pastry and arrange the lattice strips across the pie in a star shape, almost marking out the portions, pressing down the ends firmly to seal. Trim off the excess pastry and crimp the edges. Brush the pastry with milk and dredge heavily with more sugar.

Set the pie on a baking sheet and bake in the preheated oven for 15 minutes. Reduce the oven temperature to 180°C (350°F) Gas 4 and bake for a further 30–40 minutes until the pastry is golden brown and the juices bubbling all over.

rhubarb meringue pie

With the subtle sharpness of rhubarb and the sweet, fluffy pillow of delicious meringue, this is a light, fruity classic.

Preheat the oven to 180°C (350°F) Gas 4.

Cream the butter and sugar until pale and fluffy. Add the egg yolks one by one, mixing well. Mix the flour and baking powder together, then add half to the butter mixture, mixing well. Add half the milk and mix well. Finally, add the remaining flour mixture, mix, then add the remaining milk and mix well.

Transfer the dough to the tart pan and push and press it until the base and sides are evenly covered with a layer of dough.

To make the filling, mix the rhubarb, cinnamon and 2 teaspoons of the sugar together, then spread roughly over the tart. Whisk the egg whites until they hold soft peaks, then gradually add the remaining sugar, whisking until firm. Fold in the vanilla extract. Spoon on top of the pie, making peaks as you go, and scatter the almonds over the top.

Bake in the preheated oven for 35–40 minutes.

100 g/6½ tablespoons unsalted butter, softened at room temperature

65 g/⅓ cup caster/granulated sugar

2 eggs, separated

90 g/¾ cup plain/all-purpose flour

1 teaspoon baking powder

50 ml/3 tablespoons milk

For the filling:

3–4 sticks/stalks of rhubarb, trimmed and roughly chopped

1 teaspoon ground cinnamon

65 g/⅓ cup plus 2 teaspoons caster/granulated sugar

1 teaspoon pure vanilla extract

50 g flaked/slivered almonds

a 24-cm/10-inch loose-based, fluted tart pan, greased

Serves 6–8

mango curd pavlova pie

This is an outrage of a pie! Clouds of gooey Pavlova meringue float on top of a luscious filling of fresh mango curd.

Preheat the oven to 190°F (375°C) Gas 5.

Roll out the pastry on a lightly-floured surface and use to line the pie plate. Prick the base of the pastry with a fork, line with parchment paper or kitchen foil, then fill with baking beans and bake blind (see page 11) for 15 minutes. Remove from the oven and brush the whole inside of the tart with beaten egg, then return to the oven for 5 minutes until the egg glaze has cooked. Brush and bake again if necessary, then leave to cool.

For the filling, blend the mango flesh, sugar and lime zest and juice in a food processor until smooth, scraping down the side occasionally. Add the whole eggs and egg yolks and process for a few seconds more until mixed. Strain the curd mixture through a coarse sieve/strainer into the pie crust and spread out evenly.

Reduce the oven temperature to 140°C (275°F) Gas 1.

For the topping, whisk the egg whites and salt with an electric hand-whisk until very stiff. Gradually whisk in the sugar, one large spoonful at a time, making sure the meringue is really 'bouncily' stiff before adding the next spoonful. Whisk in the cornflour/cornstarch, vanilla and vinegar. Spoon evenly over the pie, ensuring that you seal the edges with meringue. Pile this as high as you can!

Bake for about 45 minutes until the meringue is just turning palest brown. Remove the pie from the oven, cool for a few minutes then serve warm (the filling may still be a bit soft) or leave to cool completely (the filling will be firm) and serve cold.

1 quantity Rich Shortcrust Pastry (see page 14)

1 egg, beaten

For the mango curd filling:

500 g/1 lb. 2 oz. ripe mango flesh (about 2 large mangoes), chopped

125 g/⅔ cup caster/granulated sugar

finely grated zest and freshly squeezed juice of 2 limes

3 whole eggs, plus 4 egg yolks

For the Pavlova topping:

4 egg whites

a pinch of sea salt

225 g/1 cup plus 2 tablespoons caster/superfine sugar

1 teaspoon cornflour/cornstarch

1 teaspoon pure vanilla extract

1 teaspoon vinegar

a 23-cm/9-inch loose-based tart pan

Serves 6

For the pie crust:

200 g/7 oz. mixed ginger nuts and digestives/gingersnaps and graham crackers

100 g/6½ tablespoons unsalted butter

50 g/¼ cup caster/ granulated sugar

For the key lime filling:

3 large egg yolks, at room temperature

2 teaspoons finely grated lime zest

397-g/14-oz. can sweetened condensed milk

150 ml/⅔ cup freshly squeezed lime juice (from about 6 limes)

200 ml/¾ cup double/heavy cream

1 tablespoon icing/ confectioners' sugar

lime slices, to decorate

a 23-cm/9-inch tart pan, 2.5 cm/1 inch deep

Serves 8

key lime pie

A classic pie from the Florida Keys, where this recipe has been popular since the late 19th century.

Preheat the oven to 190°C (375°F) Gas 5.

Put the biscuits/cookies and crackers in a plastic bag and bash with a rolling pin until finely crushed.

Melt the butter in a saucepan, then mix in the biscuit/cookie crumbs and sugar until well coated. Spread the crumb mixture evenly over the base and up the sides of the tart pan, pressing in lightly with the back of a spoon (or a potato masher). Set on a baking sheet with a lip to catch any melting butter that may escape. Bake in the preheated oven for 8–10 minutes, then remove from the oven and let cool. Leave the oven on.

Using an electric hand whisk, beat the egg yolks and lime zest together for about 5 minutes until pale, thick and fluffy. Gradually whisk in the condensed milk and continue to whisk for a further 5 minutes until very thick and fluffy. Now whisk in the lime juice, spoonful by spoonful, keeping the mix nice and fluffy (it will thin down a bit).

Pour the filling into the cooled baked pie crust and set the pan on a baking sheet. Bake in the centre of the oven for about 15 minutes or until just set but still a bit wobbly in the centre. Transfer to a wire rack to cool for 30 minutes, cover and refrigerate for at least 2 hours.

To serve, whip the cream with the icing/confectioners' sugar until thick but spreadable (do not overwhip). Spread or pipe the cream over the top of the pie and decorate with slices of lime. Alternatively, you can just decorate with lime slices and serve with dollops of whipped cream on the side.

TIP: This freezes well for up to 3 months, minus the cream.

shoofly pie

This classic is named after the brand of molasses that published the original recipe – Shoo Fly Molasses.

Roll out the pastry on a lightly floured surface and use it to line the pie plate. Trim off the excess pastry and prick the base with a fork. Chill for 30 minutes.

Preheat the oven to 200°C (400°F) Gas 6 and set a heavy baking sheet on the middle shelf.

Line the chilled pie crust with parchment paper or kitchen foil, then fill with baking beans. Set the pie plate on the baking sheet in the preheated oven and bake blind (see page 11) for 15 minutes. Remove the parchment or foil and beans and return to the oven for a further 8–10 minutes to dry out the pastry. Remove from the oven, place on a wire rack and leave to cool.

Reduce the oven temperature to 180°C (350°F) Gas 4.

To make the crumb topping, put the flour, sugar, butter and salt into a food processor and process until it forms fairly fine crumbs (don't overprocess). Reserve 6 tablespoons and set both aside.

To make the filling, sprinkle the bicarbonate of/baking soda into a mixing bowl and pour the boiling water over it. Pour in the treacle or molasses, beaten egg and vanilla extract and whisk well with a balloon whisk to combine. Stir in the larger amount of crumbs and whisk again. Pour into the cooled pie crust and sprinkle the remaining 6 tablespoons of crumb mixture evenly over the top.

Gently set the pie on the baking sheet in the preheated oven and bake for 40–45 minutes or until the filling just begins to puff up and crack slightly. Remove from the oven and transfer to a wire rack to cool completely before serving. The filling should still be slightly moist and sticky in the centre.

1 quantity American Pie Crust (see page 16), made with half white cooking fat/shortening, half butter

For the crumb topping:

165 g/1⅓ cups plain/all-purpose flour

125 g/⅔ cup packed soft dark brown sugar

50 g/4 tablespoons unsalted butter, chilled and cubed

¼ teaspoon salt

For the molasses filling:

¾ teaspoon bicarbonate of/baking soda

175 ml/¾ cup boiling water

225 g/scant 1 cup black treacle or molasses

1 large egg, beaten

1 teaspoon pure vanilla extract

a 23-cm/9-inch metal pie plate

Serves 8–10

mississippi mud pie

A dream of a pie for any chocolate lover. The filling puffs up, then settles down and cracks as it cools to resemble the cracked and dried riverbed, but the centre is soft and velvety.

1 quantity American Pie Crust (see page 16)

75 g/5 tablespoons unsalted butter

50 g/1¾ oz. dark/bittersweet chocolate, chopped

6 tablespoons unsweetened cocoa powder, sifted

3 large eggs

250 g/1¼ cups caster/granulated sugar

2 tablespoons crème fraîche or sour cream

3 tablespoons golden syrup/light corn syrup

2 teaspoons pure vanilla extract

chocolate shavings, chocolate-covered nuts or chocolate buttons, to decorate

a 23-cm/9-inch loose-based pie plate, 3.5 cm/1½ inches deep

Serves 8

Roll out the pastry on a lightly floured surface and use to line the pie plate. Chill for 30 minutes.

Preheat the oven to 180°C (350°F) Gas 4 and set a heavy baking sheet on the middle shelf.

For the filling, melt the butter in a small saucepan. Remove from the heat and add the chocolate and cocoa powder, stirring until the chocolate is melted and the mixture is smooth. Set aside.

Whisk the eggs and sugar together until the mixture is pale and creamy, then whisk in the crème fraîche or sour cream, syrup and vanilla extract. Fold this light mixture into the chocolate mix and pour into the pie crust.

Set the pie on the baking sheet in the preheated oven and bake for 35–40 minutes or until the filling puffs up, cracks and forms a crust on top (but is still a bit wobbly in the centre). Remove from the oven and cool for 30 minutes on a wire rack.

Chill for at least 2 hours before serving decorated with chocolate shavings, chocolate-covered nuts or chocolate buttons to look like the twigs and pebbles on a riverbed.

TIP: This can be made 2 days in advance and stored in the fridge.

Whether it is the never-ending possibilities for fillings or the cosy and comforting baking smell that you get when cooking savoury tarts, there are few who would turn down the offer of a slice!

savoury tarts

quiche lorraine

A classic tart from Alsace and Lorraine, and the forerunner of many copies. Made well and with the best ingredients, this simplest of dishes is food fit for the gods.

1 recipe Basic Shortcrust Pastry
(see pages 12–13)

200 g/8 oz. bacon, chopped

5 medium eggs

200 ml/¾ cup double/heavy
cream or crème fraîche

freshly grated nutmeg, to taste

50 g/½ cup Gruyère cheese,
grated

sea salt and freshly ground
black pepper

a 23 cm/9 inch tart pan

foil or parchment paper

baking beans

Serves 4–6

Bring the Basic Shortcrust Pastry to room temperature. Preheat the oven to 200°C (400°F) Gas 6.

Roll out the pastry thinly on a lightly floured work surface and use to line the tart pan. Prick the base and then chill or freeze it for 15 minutes.

Blind bake the tart base by following the instructions on page 11.

Heat a non-stick frying pan/skillet and fry the bacon until brown and crisp, then drain on paper towels. Scatter over the base of the pastry case.

Put the eggs and cream or crème fraîche into a bowl, beat well, and season with salt, pepper and nutmeg to taste. Carefully pour the mixture over the bacon and sprinkle with the Gruyère cheese.

Bake for about 25 minutes until just set, golden brown and puffy. Serve warm or at room temperature.

goats' cheese, leek and walnut tart

This light, creamy open tart is easy to make because there is no need to line a pan or bake blind – simply roll out the pastry and top like a pizza.

½ recipe Puff Pastry (see page 15) or 250 g/9 oz. frozen puff pastry, thawed

50 g/4 tablespoons butter

4 small leeks, trimmed and sliced

200 g/8 oz. goats' cheese log with rind, sliced

sea salt and freshly ground black pepper

125 g/1¼ cups walnut pieces

3 garlic cloves, crushed

6 tablespoons walnut oil

3 tablespoons chopped fresh flat-leaf parsley, plus extra to serve

a 28 cm/11 inch dinner plate

Serves 4–6

Preheat the oven to 200°C (400°F) Gas 6. Roll out the pastry thinly on a lightly floured work surface and cut out a 28 cm/11 inch circle using the dinner plate as a template. Set on a baking sheet and chill or freeze for at least 15 minutes.

Melt the butter in a large saucepan and add the leeks, stirring to coat. Add a few tablespoons of water and a teaspoon of salt, and cover with a lid. Steam very gently for at least 20 minutes (trying not to look too often!) until almost soft. Remove the lid and cook for a few minutes to evaporate any excess liquid. Let cool.

To make the walnut paste, blend the walnuts and garlic in a food processor with 2 tablespoons water. Beat in the walnut oil and stir in the parsley. Spread this over the pastry, avoiding the rim.

Spoon the leeks into the pastry base and top with the slices of goats' cheese. Sprinkle with any remaining walnut paste. Season with salt and freshly ground black pepper and sprinkle with olive oil. Bake for 20 minutes until the pastry is golden and the cheese bubbling and brown.

Sprinkle with more parsley and serve immediately.

potato and parmesan tart with chives

Real comfort food for a miserable wet weekend! This is a deliciously creamy tart, which makes an unusual supper dish served with smoked salmon or a crunchy Caesar salad.

1 recipe Rich Shortcrust Pastry (see page 14)

900 g/2 lbs. white potatoes, thinly sliced

50 g/4 tablespoons butter, cut into pieces

125 g/1¼ cups freshly grated Parmesan cheese

4 tablespoons chopped chives

freshly grated nutmeg, to taste

1 medium egg, beaten

300 ml/1¼ cups double/heavy cream

sea salt and freshly ground black pepper

a deep loose-based tart pan, 21 cm/8 inches in diameter or any suitable dish with a 1 litre/quart capacity

foil or parchment paper

baking beans

Serves 4–6

Bring the pastry to room temperature. Preheat the oven to 200°C (400°F) Gas 6.

Roll out the pastry thinly on a lightly floured work surface. Use the pastry to line the pan or dish (this can be a little tricky, so be patient and take your time), then prick the base. Chill or freeze for 15 minutes, then blind bake the tart base by following the instructions on page 11.

After blind baking, turn down the oven to 160°C (325°F) Gas 3. Reserve 50 g/¼ cup of the Parmesan cheese. Layer the sliced potatoes and butter in the baked case, seasoning each layer with the remaining Parmesan, chives, nutmeg, salt and pepper.

Put the egg and cream into a bowl, beat well, then pour over the potatoes. Sprinkle the reserved 50 g/¼ cup of Parmesan cheese over the top. Bake for about 1 hour (it may take up to 15 minutes longer, depending on the type of potato used) or until the potatoes are tender and the top is dark golden brown.

Let cool for 10 minutes, then remove from the pan or dish. Alternatively, serve straight from the dish!

TIP: Do not rinse the potatoes – their starch will help to thicken the cream.

asparagus tart

This gluten-free tart will keep for up to 3 days in the fridge in an airtight container or covered in clingfilm/plastic wrap.

Trim any woody ends from the asparagus spears, then blanch them in a pan of boiling, salted water for about 3 minutes until just soft. Plunge into iced water and leave until you are ready to fill the tart.

To make the pastry, rub the butter into the flour using your fingertips, then add the cream cheese and salt and bring together into a soft ball of dough, adding 1–2 tablespoons water if the mixture is too dry. Wrap the pastry dough in clingfilm/plastic wrap and chill in the refrigerator for 1 hour.

On a flour-dusted surface, roll out the pastry to 2–3 mm/⅛ inch thick and use it to line the tart pan. Press the pastry in firmly with your fingers and trim away any excess using a sharp knife. If the pastry breaks, don't worry, just patch any holes with the pastry trimmings. Prick the base and chill in the refrigerator for 30 minutes.

Preheat the oven to 180°C (350°F) Gas 4.

Line the pastry case with non-stick parchment paper, fill with baking beans and bake for about 15–20 minutes until the pastry is golden brown. Remove the tart case from the oven and leave to cool slightly. Remove the parchment paper and baking beans. Turn the oven temperature down to 120°C (250°F) Gas ½.

Whisk together the egg yolks, cream and lemon zest and season with salt and pepper, then slowly pour the mixture into the pastry case. Arrange the asparagus spears in a decorative pattern in the tart. They will sink into the filling slightly but will still be visible on top. Carefully transfer the tart to the oven and bake for about 1½ hours until the top of the tart is lightly golden brown and the filling is just set with a slight wobble in the centre. Leave to cool, then chill in the refrigerator until you are ready to serve.

For the pastry:

75 g/5 tablespoons butter, chilled and cubed

190 g/1½ cups gluten-free plain/all-purpose flour, sifted, plus extra for dusting

75 g/5 tablespoons cream cheese

¼ teaspoon salt

For the filling:

250 g/9 oz. asparagus

5 egg yolks

300 ml/1¼ cups whipping cream

grated zest of 1 lemon

sea salt and ground black pepper

a 30 x 18-cm/12 x 7-inch loose-based tart pan, greased

baking beans

Serves 8

1 recipe Rich Shortcrust Pastry (see page 14)

75 g/6 tablespoons unsalted butter

1 onion, sliced

450 g/1 lb. portobello mushrooms, sliced

freshly squeezed juice of 1 lemon

2 tablespoons chopped fresh tarragon

200 g/8 oz. mascarpone cheese, softened

3 large eggs, beaten

sea salt and freshly ground black pepper

For the garlic crunch topping:

55 g/4 tablespoons butter

150 g/1 cup stale breadcrumbs

3 garlic cloves, chopped

finely grated zest of 1 unwaxed lemon

3 tablespoons chopped fresh flat-leaf parsley

a deep, fluted tart pan, 25 cm/ 10 inches diameter

foil or parchment paper

baking beans

Serves 6–8

portobello mushroom and tarragon tart

Portobello mushrooms are full of flavour – the darker, the better. This tart has a creamy filling laced with tarragon and lemon. The garlicky crunchy topping turns it into a giant version of a stuffed mushroom – but more sophisticated!

Bring the pastry to room temperature. Preheat the oven to 200°C (400°F) Gas 6.

Roll out the pastry thinly on a lightly floured work surface. Use to line the tart pan, then chill or freeze for 15 minutes. Blind bake the tart case following the instructions on page 11.

Melt the butter in a frying pan/skillet, add the onion and fry until soft and golden. Add the mushrooms, lemon juice, salt and pepper, then fry over a medium heat for 5 minutes until the mushrooms are tender and the liquid has evaporated. Stir in the tarragon, then let the mixture cool slightly.

To make the topping, melt the butter in a frying pan/skillet, add the breadcrumbs, garlic, lemon zest and parsley and fry over a high heat until the breadcrumbs begin to crisp but not colour too much. Tip the mixture into a bowl.

Put the mascarpone and eggs into a bowl and beat well. Stir in the mushroom mixture. Pour into the pie/pastry case, then sprinkle with the topping and bake for 20–25 minutes until set, crisp and golden on top. Serve warm.

honey-roast parsnip, carrot and shallot tart

Plenty of roasted winter vegetables with a hint of honey set in a light spelt and olive oil crust – this makes a great rustic appetizer or accompaniment to winter roasts and stews.

3 medium carrots, sliced on the diagonal

3 medium parsnips, cut into matchsticks

6 medium shallots, quartered

1 tablespoon runny honey

40 ml/3 tablespoons olive oil

1 teaspoon salt

½ teaspoon crushed black pepper

100 g/1 cup Cheddar or other hard, sharp cheese, grated

150 g/⅔ cup Greek yogurt

For the spelt pizza dough base:

220 g/1⅔ cups spelt flour

1 teaspoon dried quick/quick-acting dry yeast

½ teaspoon salt

2 tablespoons olive oil

1 egg

60 ml/¼ cup warm water

a 23-cm/9 inch loose-based tart pan, greased

Serves 8

Preheat the oven to 200°C (400°F) Gas 6.

Put the carrots, parsnips and shallots in a roasting pan. Add the honey, oil, salt and pepper and toss until evenly coated. Cover the pan with aluminium foil and roast in the preheated oven for 30 minutes. Remove from the oven, leave covered, and leave to cool for 10–15 minutes. Reduce the oven temperature to 170°C (325°F) Gas 3.

To make the pastry, mix the flour, yeast and salt in a bowl. Make a well in the centre and pour in the oil, egg and water. Draw everything together with your hands until you get a soft dough.

Transfer the dough to a lightly floured surface and knead for a couple of minutes. The dough should be soft but not sticky. If it is sticky, add a little flour and knead again. Roll out the dough with a rolling pin until 3 mm/⅛ inch thick. Line the tart pan with the dough but do not trim the edges yet.

Mix 60 g/⅔ cup of the cheese into the roasted vegetables.

Mix together the yogurt and remaining cheese in a bowl, then spoon into the tart crust.

Scatter the roasted vegetables over the yogurt, spreading them evenly. Now trim the excess pizza dough around the edges.

Bake in the hot oven for 25–30 minutes. Remove from the oven and leave to cool.

herbed courgette and ricotta cheese tart

Filo/phyllo pastry does have a tendency to become a bit soggy, but cooking this tart in a metal cake pan and sitting it on a preheated baking sheet in the oven goes some way to solving the problem.

2 tablespoons olive oil

4–5 courgettes/zucchini, grated

4 shallots, chopped

1 handful of finely shredded fresh basil leaves

1 handful of finely shredded fresh mint leaves

2 tablespoons finely chopped fresh dill

6 sheets of filo/phyllo pastry, thawed if frozen

50 g/3 tablespoons butter, melted

200 g/7 oz. fresh ricotta cheese

3 eggs, lightly beaten

185 ml/¾ cup single/light cream

a 20-cm/8-inch square, non-stick cake pan

Serves 6

Put the oil in a frying pan/skillet set over high heat. Add the courgettes/zucchini and cook for 10 minutes, stirring often, until they start to brown. Transfer to a bowl and add the shallots and herbs. Stir to combine and set aside to cool.

Take a sheet of filo/phyllo and lightly brush it all over with some of the melted butter. Fold it in half, brush the top lightly with butter and lay the filo/phyllo in the cake pan, gently pressing it down onto the base and sides. Repeat with the remaining sheets of filo, stacking one on top of the other in the pan, until you have used them all. Cover with a clean, damp dish towel to keep the pastry moist.

Preheat the oven to 180°C (350°F) Gas 4 and put a baking sheet on the centre shelf of the oven to heat. Put the ricotta, eggs and cream in a large bowl and add the courgette/zucchini mixture. Stir well to combine, then spoon the mixture into the cake pan. Place the pan on the hot baking sheet and bake in the preheated oven for about 30–35 minutes, until the filo/phyllo is golden brown and crisp.

Let the tart cool for 10 minutes before cutting it into squares and serving warm or at room temperature.

broccoli and chorizo tart

A vibrant and surprisingly healthy dairy-free tart!

For the pastry:

225 g/1¾ cups white spelt flour

pinch of sea salt

50 g/3 tablespoons dairy-free butter, e.g. sunflower spread

60 g/¼ cup hard white vegetable shortening (it is crucial that you get the hardest one you can find)

1 egg, beaten together with 1 teaspoon water

For the filling:

3 leeks, finely chopped

1 onion, sliced

3 garlic cloves, crushed

sea salt and freshly ground black pepper

10 spears of sprouting broccoli, bases trimmed

100 g/3½ oz. good chorizo, skinned and chopped (omit for a vegetarian option)

3 eggs

100 ml/6 tablespoons soy cream/creamer

extra virgin olive oil

a 20-cm/8-inch tart pan

baking beans

Serves 8–10

Sift the flour and salt into a large bowl. Add the butter and shortening and cut into small chunks with a knife. With your hands high, rub the butter and shortening into the flour until it resembles breadcrumbs. Add a tablespoon of the egg mixture and fork the mixture together. Bring the dough together with your hands to a smooth ball. Flatten into a round, wrap in clingfilm/plastic wrap and refrigerate until cold. Preheat the oven to 180°C (350°F) Gas 4.

Roll out the pastry until 1 cm/⅜ inch thick. To line the tart pan, remove the top layer of film/wrap and roll the pastry over your rolling pin with the bottom sheet of film/wrap still on it. Lay the sheet of pastry over the pan with the film/wrap now uppermost. Remove the film/wrap. Prick the base with a fork. Line the pastry shell with parchment paper and fill with baking beans. Blind-bake in the preheated oven for about 20 minutes. (Leave the oven on.) Remove the paper and beans and brush the base and sides of the shell with the remaining egg mixture. Return to the oven and bake for a further 5–10 minutes until the base is beginning to brown. Remove and cool on a wire rack.

Heat 3 tablespoons oil in a large saucepan over medium heat. Add the leeks, onion, garlic and a good pinch of salt and pepper and sweat out until completely soft and translucent. About 10 minutes before they are done, add the broccoli. Heat another pan over medium heat. Add the chorizo and cook until a little crispy and the fat has seeped out. Add to the leek and broccoli and combine. Season to taste. Preheat the oven to 200°C (400°F) Gas 6.

Add the cooked mixture to the blind-baked tart shell, reserving a little of the mixture for the top of the tart. Beat the eggs together with the cream and pour into the tart shell. Scatter the reserved ingredients over the top. Bake the tart in the preheated oven until the top has browned a little and is firm – 30–35 minutes or so depending on your oven.

250 g/1⅔ cups plain/all-purpose flour

½ teaspoon salt

125 g/1 stick butter, chilled

1 egg yolk

1 tablespoon chilled water

For the salmon filling:

25 g/2 tablespoons butter

1 shallot, finely chopped

2 tablespoons plain/all-purpose flour

300 ml/1½ cups milk

2 large egg yolks

275 g/10 oz. cooked salmon, flaked with a fork

2 tablespoons chopped fresh dill

1 teaspoon horseradish

1 tablespoon lime juice

sea salt and freshly ground black pepper

For the lime Hollandaise sauce:

3 tablespoons white wine vinegar

3 black peppercorns

1 bay leaf

1 blade of mace

1 large egg yolk

75 g/6 tablespoons butter

grated zest and juice of 1 lime

sea salt

a 20-cm/8-inch tart pan

foil and baking beans

Serves 6

salmon and dill tart

This delicious, tangy tart is a great option for a light lunch at home or even as the centrepiece of a picnic.

To make the pastry, put the flour, salt and butter in a food processor and blend until it looks like fine breadcrumbs. Mix the egg yolk in a bowl with 1 tablespoon chilled water, add to the food processor and blend until it just starts coming together. Tip out onto a board and knead until smooth. Wrap in clingfilm/plastic wrap and chill for 30 minutes.

Meanwhile, to make the filling, melt the butter in a saucepan, add the shallot and cook until soft. Add the flour and cook for 30 seconds. Stir in the milk and bring to the boil, stirring all the time. Simmer for 2 minutes then remove from the heat and let cool.

Roll out the pastry on a floured board and use to line the pan. Prick the base with a fork and line with a square of foil. Fill with baking beans or rice, transfer to a baking sheet and bake in a preheated oven at 190° (375°F) Gas 5 for 10 minutes. Remove the foil and beans.

Beat the egg yolks into the sauce and stir in the salmon, dill or parsley, horseradish and lime juice to taste. Season well. Spoon the filling into the tart and bake at the same temperature for 25 minutes until set.

Meanwhile to make the hollandaise, put the vinegar, peppercorns, bay leaf and mace into a small saucepan and bring to the boil. Boil until reduced to 1 tablespoon. Beat the egg yolk in a bowl with a pinch of salt and 15 g/1 tablespoon of the butter. Set the bowl over a saucepan of simmering water and beat until slightly thickened. Strain in the vinegar, then beat in the remaining butter bit by bit until the sauce has thickened. Stir in the lime zest and season with salt, pepper and lime juice. Spread the hollandaise over the tart and cook under a hot grill/broiler just until browned.

quiche with smoked fish

Haddock works really well in this quiche, but you can replace it with any smoked fish, such as cold smoked salmon. Serve the quiche hot or warm, with a green salad.

200 g/2 sticks minus 2 tabelspoons unsalted butter, softened at room temperature

50 ml/3½ tablespoons crème fraîche/sour cream

150 g/1 cup plus 2 tablespoons white strong/bread flour

1 teaspoon baking powder

a pinch of salt

1 tablespoon rapeseed or vegetable oil

2 medium leeks, trimmed, cleaned and thinly sliced

3 eggs

150 ml/⅔ cup single/light cream

100 g/1 cup Cheddar or other hard, sharp cheese, grated

small bunch fresh dill, finely chopped

200 g/6½ oz. smoked haddock, boned and cut into 1-cm/½-inch cubes

a 26-cm/10-inch loose-based, fluted tart pan, greased

Serves 6–8

Make the pastry, by creaming the butter and crème fraîche/sour cream in a mixing bowl. In a separate bowl, mix the flour, baking powder and salt. Tip into the mixing bowl and mix until a dough forms. Roll into a ball, then flatten into a disc before wrapping in clingfilm/plastic wrap. Refrigerate for at least 2 hours.

Preheat the oven to 200°C (400°F) Gas 6.

Take the pastry out of the refrigerator and leave to soften for a few minutes. Do not let it come to room temperature, though.

To make the filling, heat the oil in a frying pan/skillet over low–medium heat. Stir in the leeks and cook for a few minutes until nearly soft. Set aside.

Put the eggs, cream, cheese and dill in a mixing bowl and season with salt and black pepper. Mix well.

Remove the clingfilm/plastic wrap from the pastry. Roll the pastry out on a lightly floured surface until it is slightly larger than the tart pan. Gently roll the pastry around the rolling pin and transfer it to the tart pan. Line the pan with the pastry, pressing it into the fluted edges of the pan and neatly cutting off the excess pastry.

Sprinkle the leek and smoked fish into the pastry case, then pour the cream mixture on top. If you have some dough left over, cut thin ribbons from it and arrange them on top of the quiche.

Bake in the preheated oven for 25–30 minutes, or until the pastry is golden brown.

Discover a selection of gloriously fresh and fruity tarts including Tarte Tartin and Rhubarb Tart to the deliciously decadent Dark Chocolate Mousse Tart and Pecan and Chocolate Tart with Maple Syrup.

sweet tarts

simple apple tart

Quick to make and great to eat, this recipe offers a delicious solution if you've got a few too many apples. A dollop of vanilla ice cream or whipped cream makes it a real treat.

100 g/6½ tablespoons unsalted butter, softened at room temperature

85 g/scant ½ cup caster/granulated sugar

1 egg, lightly beaten

100 g/¾ cup plain/all-purpose flour

60 g/½ cup wholemeal/ whole-wheat flour

1 teaspoon baking powder

vanilla ice cream or whipped cream, to serve

For the filling:

2 large cooking apples (about 300 g/10 oz. in weight once peeled and cored), peeled, cored and thinly sliced

1 tablespoon caster/granulated sugar

1 tablespoon ground cinnamon

a 24-cm/10-inch loose-based, fluted tart pan, greased

Serves 6–8

Preheat the oven to 200°C (400°F) Gas 6.

Put the butter and sugar in a mixing bowl and beat until well mixed. Gradually add the egg, mixing well. Tip in the flours and baking powder and mix again until a dough has formed.

Transfer the dough to the tart pan and push and press it into the pan until the base and sides are evenly covered with a neat layer of dough.

To make the filling, put the sliced apples, sugar and cinnamon in a bowl and mix together until the apples are evenly coated, then transfer to the pastry case and spread roughly, or arrange neatly in a pattern over the base of the tart.

Bake in the preheated oven for 25 minutes, or until golden brown. Remove from the oven, leave to cool slightly, then serve with vanilla ice cream or whipped cream.

tarte tatin

It's a bit of a performance to make this classic French upside-down dessert, but well worth the effort.

1 quantity Pate Sucrée (page 17, but you won't need all of it, so freeze any excess for another time), at room temperature

For the filling:

4–6 apples, peeled, cored and quartered

70 g/5 tablespoons salted butter

140 g/¾ cup caster/granulated sugar

½ teaspoon ground cinnamon

24-cm/10-inch flameproof tart pan or heavy-based, ovenproof omelette pan

Serves 8

Preheat the oven to 180°C (350°F) Gas 4.

To make the filling, put the butter, sugar and 1 tablespoon water in the flameproof tart pan or heavy-based, ovenproof omelette pan over low heat. Heat, stirring occasionally, and when the mixture begins to give off a lovely caramel scent and turns golden, remove from the heat (this can take up to 10 minutes). Arrange the apples in the caramel in concentric circles, curved side down. Take extra care at this stage and as a safety precaution have a bowl of cold water ready to dip fingers in, should any hot caramel stick to them.

Return the pan to the heat. Allow to simmer gently for about 15 minutes, watching the pan carefully to ensure the heat is not too high, which can cause the apples to stick to the pan and burn. Remove from the heat when the apples are soft and well soaked in caramel.

Roll out the pastry on a lightly floured surface to form a circle about 5 cm/2 inches larger than the pan and about 4 mm/⅛ inch thick. Carefully place the pastry over the caramelized apples, and pinch the edges to the outside of the pan. Bake in the preheated oven for 35–40 minutes until the pastry turns golden brown. Remove from the oven and trim the excess pastry from the outside of the dish. Allow to stand for 5 minutes. Cover the pan with a serving plate. Ensuring your wrists are protected from any splashes of caramel, grip the plate and dish firmly together and turn them over so that the plate is on the bottom. Give it a gentle shake before carefully lifting the pan clear of the plate. The tart is best eaten on the day of baking but will keep for 2–3 days.

blueberry tart with rye

This popular tart is a simple and attractive option for the end of a casual meal with friends.

Preheat the oven to 200°C (400°F) Gas 6.

Put the butter and sugar in a mixing bowl and beat until well mixed. Gradually add the egg, mixing well. Tip in the flours and baking powder and mix again until a dough has formed.

Transfer the dough to the pan and press it into the pan until the base and sides are evenly covered with a neat layer of dough.

To make the filling, put the crème fraîche or double/heavy cream, sour cream, egg, sugar and vanilla extract in a mixing bowl and mix well. Pour into the pastry case, then scatter the blueberries into the tart.

Bake in the preheated oven for 25 minutes, or until the filling has set and the pastry is golden brown.

100 g/6 ½ tablespoons unsalted butter, softened at room temperature

85 g/scant ½ cup caster/granulated sugar

1 egg, lightly beaten

100 g/¾ cup plain/all-purpose flour

60 g/½ cup wholemeal/dark rye flour

1 teaspoon baking powder

For the filling:

100 g/⅓ cup crème fraîche or double/heavy cream

150 ml/⅔ cup sour cream

1 egg, lightly beaten

40 g caster/granulated sugar

1 teaspoon vanilla extract

250 g/1 pint blueberries

a 24-cm/10-inch loose-based, fluted tart pan, greased

Serves 6–8

pear, almond and mascarpone tart

This recipe works best if the pears are on the overripe side so that they are fork-tender when cooked.

To make the pastry, put the flour and sugar in a food processor and pulse to combine. With the motor running, add the butter and 1–2 tablespoons cold water and mix until the mixture resembles coarse breadcrumbs and starts to gather in lumps. Transfer to a lightly-floured work surface and briefly knead to form a ball. Wrap in clingfilm/plastic wrap and chill for 1 hour, until firm.

Preheat the oven to 180°C (350°F) Gas 4.

Coarsely grate the chilled pastry into a large bowl. Using lightly floured hands, scatter the grated pastry into the prepared tart pan and use your fingers to gently press it in until the entire base and the side of the pan are covered. Bake in the preheated oven for about 25 minutes, until lightly golden. Let cool.

Peel, halve and core the pears. Put them in a non-reactive bowl with the lemon juice and 1 tablespoon of the sugar. Put the remaining sugar in a food processor. Add the mascarpone, egg and flour and process to form a thick paste. Spread the mixture over the pastry. Arrange the pears on top and scatter with the almonds and caster/granulated sugar. Bake in the still-hot oven for 40–45 minutes, until the pears are soft and the mascarpone mixture has set. Serve in slices with cream or vanilla ice cream.

4 very ripe pears

1 tablespoon freshly squeezed lemon juice

6 tablespoons caster/granulated sugar

125 g/½ cup mascarpone

1 egg

1 tablespoon plain/all-purpose flour

100 g/⅔ cup flaked/slivered almonds

chilled cream or vanilla ice cream, to serve

For the pastry:

200 g/1½ cups plain/all-purpose flour

4 tablespoons caster/granulated sugar

80 g/5½ tablespoons unsalted butter, chilled and cubed

a 24-cm/10-inch loose-based, fluted tart pan, greased and floured

Serves 8–10

fresh raspberry and almond tart

This tart tastes better the day after it's made, which makes it ideal for preparing ahead of time.

150 g/5 oz. fresh raspberries, frozen until firm

1 egg

3 tablespoons caster/granulated sugar

1 tablespoon plain/all-purpose flour

75 g/5 tablespoons unsalted butter

chilled cream, to serve (optional)

For the almond shortcrust pastry:

50 g/⅓ cup almonds

200 g/1½ cups plain/all-purpose flour

80 g/7 tablespoons caster/granulated sugar

125 g/1 stick unsalted butter, chilled and cubed

a rectangular tart pan, 37 x 10 cm 5 x 8 inches, lightly greased

Serves 6–8

Preheat the oven to 180°C (350°F) Gas 4.

To make the pastry, put the almonds, flour and sugar in a food processor and process until the almonds are finely ground. With the motor running, add a cube of butter at a time until it is all incorporated and the mixture resembles coarse breadcrumbs. Add 2 tablespoons cold water and process until just combined. Be careful not to overprocess.

Tip the pastry out onto a lightly-floured work surface and knead to form a ball. Roll it out between 2 layers of parchment paper until it is about 5 cm/2 inches longer and 5 cm/2 inches wider than the tart pan. Carefully lift the pastry into the pan and use your fingers to press it down into the base and sides, letting it overhang. Prick the base all over with a fork and bake in the preheated oven for 20 minutes, until lightly golden. Break off the overhanging pastry.

Put the egg, sugar and flour in a bowl and use a balloon whisk to beat until thick and pale. Put the butter in a small saucepan and set over medium heat. Let melt until frothy and dark golden with a nutty aroma. Working quickly, pour the melted butter over the egg mixture and beat well. Scatter the raspberries in the tart case. Pour the warm batter over the raspberries. Bake in the still-hot oven for about 45 minutes, until the top resembles a golden meringue. Let cool for 30 minutes before serving. Cut into slices and serve with chilled cream, if liked.

tarte au citron

This classic French-style dessert is so popular that it's practically a permanent fixture on the menu. Simple and easy to make, it has a satisfyingly subtle lemon flavour and a wonderful melt-in-the-mouth, creamy texture.

1 quantity Pate Sablée (see page 17 but you won't need all of it, so freeze any excess for another time), chilled

For the filling:

3 eggs, plus 1 egg yolk

150 g/¾ cup caster/granulated sugar

135 ml/½ cup plus 1 tablespoon double/heavy cream

grated zest and freshly squeezed juice of 3 lemons

icing/confectioners' sugar, to dust (optional)

23-cm/9-inch loose-based fluted tart pan

parchment paper

baking beans

chef's blowtorch (optional)

Serves 10–12

Preheat the oven to 190°C (375°F) Gas 5.

Roll out the chilled pastry on a lightly floured surface to form a circle about 30 cm/12 inches in diameter and about 3 mm/⅛ inch thick. Drape the pastry over the rolling pin and carefully transfer it to the tart pan. Gently mould the pastry into the base and sides. The pastry is fragile to handle but any gaps can be repaired using surplus pastry. Trim the top edge with a sharp knife. Prick the base in a few places with a fork and line the tart case with a sheet of baking parchment. Fill the tart case with baking beans and blind bake in the preheated oven for 15–20 minutes. Take out of the oven, remove the baking parchment and baking beans and return to the oven for another 5 minutes to lightly colour the pastry. Remove from the oven and reduce the oven temperature to 180°C (350°F) Gas 4.

To make the filling, put the eggs, egg yolk, sugar, cream and lemon zest and juice into a large bowl. Lightly whisk, then transfer to a saucepan set over low–medium heat. Heat gently, stirring constantly, until starts to thicken. Be careful not to over heat otherwise it can curdle. Put the tart pan on a baking sheet and carefully pour the filling into the tart case. Bake for 15 minutes or until just set. Allow to cool completely before removing from the tart pan. If you choose, you can lightly brown the surface of tart using a chef's blowtorch or simply dust with icing/confectioners' sugar before serving.

Well wrapped, the tart will keep for 3–5 days in the refrigerator.

free-form caramelized peach tart

So simple and so good – especially with all-butter homemade pastry and when peaches are at their very best.

1 recipe Puff Pastry (see page 15)

4–6 ripe peaches

55 g/5 tablespoons butter

freshly squeezed juice of ½ lemon

150 g/1 cup caster/granulated sugar

whipped cream or crème fraîche, to serve

a dinner plate, 28 cm/11 inches in diameter (to use as a template)

Serves 6

Preheat the oven to 230°C (450°F) Gas 8.

Roll out the pastry on a lightly floured work surface and cut out a circle with a 28 cm/11 inch diameter, using a large dinner plate as a template. Lift onto a baking sheet and make an edge by twisting the pastry over itself all the way around the edge. Press lightly to seal. Still on the baking sheet, chill or freeze for at least 15 minutes.

Peel the peaches if necessary, then halve and pit them and cut into chunky slices. Put the butter into a saucepan, then add the lemon juice and half the sugar. Heat until melted, then add the peaches and toss gently. Pile the peaches all over the pastry in a casual way. Sprinkle with the remaining sugar and bake in the preheated oven for 20–25 minutes until golden, puffed and caramelized. Serve with whipped cream or crème fraîche.

rhubarb tart

The base for this tart is a lovely cross between crust and biscuit/cookie. When you mix the dough, it will feel wet, but that is how it should be – just flour your hands before you press the dough into the tart pan.

150 g/1 cup plus 3 tablespoons plain/all-purpose flour

1 teaspoon baking powder

100 g/6½ tablespoons unsalted butter, softened at room temperature and diced

85 g/scant ½ cup caster/granulated sugar

1 egg yolk

For the filling:

300 g/10 oz. rhubarb, trimmed and roughly chopped

2 tablespoons dark brown soft sugar

50 g/3 tablespoons unsalted butter, softened at room temperature and diced

60 g/⅓ cup caster/granulated sugar

50 g porridge/old-fashioned oats

a 20-cm/8-inch loose-based, fluted tart pan, greased

Serves 6–8

Preheat the oven to 200°C (400°F) Gas 6.

Sift the flour and baking powder into a mixing bowl. Rub the butter into the flour mixture with your fingertips until it looks like breadcrumbs. Stir in the sugar and egg yolk and mix until a dough forms.

Transfer the dough to the tart pan and push and press it into the pan until the base and sides are evenly covered with a neat layer of dough.

To make the filling, put the rhubarb and brown sugar in a bowl and mix until the rhubarb is evenly coated, then transfer to the pastry case and spread roughly over the base of the tart.

In a separate bowl, mix the butter, caster/granulated sugar and oats together until until you have a rough, crumbly mixture. Scatter roughly over the rhubarb filling.

Bake in the preheated oven for 30 minutes, or until the crumble topping and pastry are golden brown.

treacle tart

This is such a nostalgia trip; a good old-fashioned British dessert. This polished version is made with sweet crumbly pastry and zest of lemon.

1 quantity Pâte Sablée (see page 17 but you won't need all of it, so freeze any excess for another time), chilled

For the filling:

100 g/1 cup breadcrumbs

60 g/½ cup ground almonds

1 egg, lightly beaten

125 ml/½ cup single/light cream

a pinch of ground ginger

grated zest of 1 lemon

340 g/1½ cups golden syrup/light corn syrup

25 g/½ cup corn flakes, crushed

a 23-cm/9-inch loose-based fluted tart pan

baking beans

Serves 8–10

Preheat the oven to 190°C (375°F) Gas 5.

Roll out the chilled pastry on a lightly floured surface to form a circle about 30 cm/12 inches in diameter and about 3 mm/⅛ inch thick. Drape the pastry over the rolling pin and carefully transfer it to the tart pan. Gently mould the pastry into the base and sides. The pastry is fragile to handle but any gaps can be repaired using surplus pastry. Trim the top edge with a sharp knife. Line the tart case with a sheet of baking parchment. Fill the tart case with baking beans and blind bake in the preheated oven for 15–20 minutes. Take out of the oven, remove the baking parchment and baking beans and return to the oven for another 5 minutes to lightly colour the pastry. Remove from the oven and reduce the oven temperature to 160°C (325°F) Gas 3.

To make the filling, put the breadcrumbs, ground almonds, egg, cream, ginger and lemon zest into a large bowl and stir together. Warm the syrup in a saucepan, then add it to the mixture in the bowl and blend together.

Spoon the mixture into the tart case, place the tart on a baking sheet and bake in the preheated oven for 20 minutes. Remove from the oven and sprinkle the corn flakes over the tart. Return to the oven and bake for a further 30 minutes. Remove from the oven and allow to cool in the pan.

The tart will keep for up to 7 days in an airtight container.

walnut tart with quick fudge ice cream

This soft, sticky tart packed with walnuts is superb with the easy vanilla ice cream marbled with fudge toffee.

1 recipe Rich Shortcrust Pastry (see page 14)

For the walnut filling:

125 g/1 stick unsalted butter, softened

125 g/½ cup plus 2 tablespoons light soft brown sugar

3 large eggs

grated zest and juice of 1 small orange

175 g/¾ cup golden/light corn syrup

225 g/2½ cups walnut pieces, coarsely chopped

a pinch of salt

For the quick fudge/taffy ice cream:

150 g/6 oz. chewy toffees/taffy

100 g/1 cup double/heavy cream

600 ml/1 pint best quality vanilla ice cream, softened

a 23 cm/9 inch fluted tart pan

Serves 6

Bring the pastry to room temperature. Preheat the oven to 190°C (375°F) Gas 5.

Roll out the pastry on a lightly floured work surface and use to line the tart pan. Prick the base and chill or freeze for 15 minutes, then bake blind following the instructions on page 11. Take the tart base out of the oven and let cool. Lower the oven temperature to 180°C (350°F) Gas 4.

To make the filling, put the butter and sugar into a bowl and cream until light and fluffy. Gradually beat in the eggs, one at a time. Beat the orange zest and juice into the butter and egg mixture. Heat the golden/light corn syrup in a small saucepan until runny, but not very hot. Stir into the butter mixture, then stir in the walnuts and salt.

Pour into the pastry case and bake for 45 minutes until lightly browned and risen. The tart will sink a little on cooling.

While the tart is cooling, make the ice cream. Put the toffees/taffy and double/heavy cream into a small saucepan and stir over a medium heat to melt. Cool slightly and stir quickly into the ice cream so that it looks marbled. Put the ice cream back in the freezer until ready to serve.

Serve the tart at room temperature with scoops of the fudge/taffy ice cream.

pecan and chocolate tart with maple syrup

Genuine maple syrup has a unique kind of sweetness that adds something extra to this rather decadent dish. Best saved for a special occasion, it's very rich and a little goes a long way.

1 quantity Pate Sucrée (see page 17), chilled

For the filling:

200 g/¾ cup maple syrup

20 g/1½ cups muscovado sugar

20 g/1½ tablespoons salted butter

80 g/2½ oz. dark/bittersweet chocolate, finely chopped

3 eggs

150 g/1 cup pecan halves

a 23-cm/9-inch loose-based fluted tart pan

baking beans

Serves 10–12

Preheat the oven to 190°C (375°F) Gas 5.

Roll out the chilled pastry on a lightly floured surface to form a circle about 30 cm/12 inches in diameter and about 3 mm/⅛ inch thick. Drape the pastry over the rolling pin and carefully transfer it to the tart pan. Gently mould the pastry into the base and sides. The pastry is fragile to handle but any gaps can be repaired using surplus pastry. Trim the top edge with a sharp knife. Prick the base in a few places with a fork and line the tart case with a sheet of baking parchment. Fill the tart case with baking beans and blind bake in the preheated oven for 15–20 minutes. Take out of the oven, remove the baking parchment and baking beans and return to the oven for another 5 minutes to lightly colour the pastry. Remove from the oven and reduce the oven temperature to 150°C (300°F) Gas 2.

To make the filling, put maple syrup, sugar and butter into a saucepan and stir over medium heat until melted. Remove from the heat and add the chocolate, stirring until it has melted and the mixture is smooth. Add the eggs and beat into the mixture. Finally, stir in the nuts.

Pour the mixture into the tart case and bake in the preheated oven for 30–35 minutes or until the filling is just set.

The tart can be served warm or at room temperature. It will keep for 2–3 days in an airtight container.

baked dark chocolate mousse tart

This is wickedly delicious. Use the darkest chocolate you can find and serve the tart in thin slices. The filling is really rich – delicious with sour cherry jam and crème fraîche.

1 recipe Pâte Sucrée
(see page 17)

For the chocolate mousse filling:

400 g/14 oz. dark/bittersweet chocolate, broken into pieces

125 g/1 stick unsalted butter, cubed

5 large eggs, separated

125 g/½ cup plus 2 tablespoons caster/granulated sugar

150 ml/⅔ cup double/heavy cream, at room temperature

3 tablespoons dark rum (optional)

icing/confectioners' sugar, to dust

single/light cream, to serve

*a deep loose-based tart pan,
25 cm/10 inches in diameter,
4 cm/1½ inches deep*

foil and baking beans

Serves 8

Bring the pastry to room temperature. Preheat the oven to 190°C (375°F) Gas 5.

Roll out the pastry thinly on a lightly floured work surface, then use to line the tart pan. Prick the base, then chill or freeze for 15 minutes.

Line with foil and baking beans and bake blind for 15 minutes. Remove the foil and beans, turn the oven down to 180°C (350°F) Gas 4 and return to the oven for 10–15 minutes to dry out and brown. Cool and remove from the pan, then transfer to a serving platter.

Put the chocolate and butter into a bowl and melt over a saucepan of simmering water. As soon as it has melted, remove the bowl from the heat and cool slightly for a minute or so.

Put the egg yolks and sugar into a bowl and whisk with an electric beater until pale and creamy. Stir the cream and the rum, if using, into the melted chocolate mixture, then quickly fold in the egg yolk mixture. Put the egg whites into a clean bowl and whisk until soft peaks form. Quickly fold into the chocolate mixture.

Pour into the pastry case and bake for 25 minutes until risen and a bit wobbly. Remove from the oven and let cool – the filling will sink and firm up as it cools. Dust with icing/confectioners' sugar, and serve at room temperature with cream.

These savoury and sweet portable pies and tartlets are perfect for entertaining friends or for making festive occasions that little bit more special.

party pies and tartlets

12 quail's eggs

225 g/8 oz. lean minced/
ground pork

100 g/3½ oz. dry-cure bacon
or pancetta, minced/ground
or finely chopped

1 small onion, grated

3 tablespoons Branston Pickle,
or spiced vegetable chutney

2 teaspoons dried mixed herbs

4 tablespoons chopped fresh
flat-leaf parsley

1 quantity Basic Shortcrust Pastry
(see pages 12–13)

1 egg, beaten with a pinch
of salt, to glaze

salt and freshly ground
black pepper

*a 9-cm/3½-inch round pastry
cutter*

*a 7-cm/2¾-inch round pastry
cutter*

a 12-hole bun/muffin pan

Makes 12

piggy pies

These wonderful little pies are a special picnic treat, but be warned: they to do tend to disappear very quickly!

Prick through the shell at the wide end of each quail's egg with a pin – this will allow the trapped air to escape and prevent the eggs cracking as they cook. Soft-boil the eggs in a pan of boiling water for 2 minutes 45 seconds. Drain, then cool under running water until completely cold. Carefully peel off the shells under cold running water and keep submerged in a bowl of cold water until ready to use.

Preheat the oven to 400°F (200°C) Gas 6.

To make the filling, put the minced/ground pork, bacon or pancetta, onion, pickle or chutney, dried herbs and parsley in a large mixing bowl. Mix using your hands or a wooden spoon and season with a little salt and plenty of pepper.

Roll out the pastry on a lightly floured surface to a thickness of about 3–4 mm/⅛ inch. Cut 12 rounds using the large pastry cutter, and 12 rounds for the lids using the smaller pastry cutter.

Carefully press and mould the larger rounds into the holes of the muffin pan, making sure they reach the top. Half-fill each with the pork filling, top with a quail's egg, then top with another layer of filling, carefully tucking it around the egg.

Brush the inside edges of each filled pie with a little beaten egg and place a lid on top, pressing the edges together to seal. Trim if necessary. Make a hole in the top of each pie (I use the tip of a metal piping nozzle/tip), brush the tops with more beaten egg and bake in the preheated oven for 20 minutes. Reduce the oven temperature to 160°C (325°F) Gas 3 and cook for a further 25–30 minutes until the pastry is golden and the filling is cooked through. Cool on a wire rack, then wrap in parchment paper and store in the fridge for up to 5 days.

2 quantities Basic Shortcrust Pastry (see pages 12–13)

2 tablespoons sunflower oil

1 onion, finely chopped

1 large orange-fleshed sweet potato, diced

2 tablespoons spicy mango chutney or sweet chilli sauce

2 tablespoons chopped fresh thyme or lemon thyme

450 g/1 lb. canned corned beef, chilled and diced

1 egg, beaten, to glaze

salt and freshly ground black pepper

a 20-cm/8-inch dinner plate

a baking sheet lined with non-stick parchment paper

Makes 6 large pasties or 12 smaller ones

corned beef and sweet potato pasties

These pasties are almost like corned beef hash in pastry. Made using orange-fleshed sweet potatoes, their sweet earthy taste contrasts nicely with the saltiness of the corned beef.

Roll out the pastry on a lightly floured surface and cut out 6 rounds, using the plate as a guide.

Heat the oil in a sauté pan and add the onion. Cook over medium heat for 5 minutes until beginning to soften. Add the sweet potato and cook, stirring from time to time, for 10 minutes or until just tender. Stir in the chutney or sweet chilli sauce and thyme and leave to cool. Once cold, fold in the corned beef and season well.

Divide the mixture between the 6 pastry circles and crimp the edges together to seal in the filling – over the top or to the side, the choice is yours! Brush with the beaten egg and chill for 30 minutes.

Preheat the oven to 200°C (400°F) Gas 6.

Arrange the chilled pasties on the prepared baking sheet, make a little steam hole in each one and bake in the preheated oven for 20–30 minutes until the pastry is golden brown. Remove from the oven and serve hot or transfer to a wire rack to cool.

2 tablespoons vegetable oil

1 small onion, diced

2 garlic cloves, crushed

1 tablespoon chopped fresh ginger

1–2 teaspoons of your favourite curry paste

2 teaspoons black mustard seeds

200 g/7 oz. floury potatoes, diced

1 small orange-fleshed sweet potato, diced

1 tablespoon palm sugar or soft brown sugar

80 g/⅔ cup frozen peas

50 g/⅓ cup roasted cashew nuts, chopped

25 g/½ cup roughly chopped fresh coriander/cilantro

2 quantities Basic Shortcrust Pastry (see pages 12–13)

vegetable oil, for deep-frying

salt and freshly ground black pepper

a 12-cm/5-inch round pastry cutter

Makes about 20

spicy vegetable samosas

These are wonderful served warm, fresh out of the fryer, or equally good eaten cold from a lunch box. Any root vegetable can be used in the filling, as long as it is cooked until really tender before filling the samosa.

Heat the ghee or oil in a large heavy-based non-stick frying pan/skillet set over medium heat. Cook the onion, garlic and ginger with the curry paste and mustard seeds for 5 minutes, stirring regularly until golden and smelling really good.

Add the potato, sweet potato and sugar. Cook, stirring regularly, for 8–10 minutes or until the potatoes are tender. Stir in the peas, reduce the heat to low, cover and steam for a further 3 minutes. Remove from the heat and let cool, then taste and season and stir in the cashews and coriander/cilantro.

Roll out the pastry on a lightly floured surface. Using the pastry cutter, cut 20 circles from the pastry. Place 1 generous tablespoon of filling in the middle of each circle. Brush the edges lightly with water to dampen, then fold the pastry over and pinch the sides together to seal firmly.

Heat the oil in a deep-fat fryer or stable wok to 170°C (325°F), or until a cube of bread browns in 20 seconds. Deep-fry 3 samosas at a time for about 3–4 minutes, turning over halfway through and cooking until crisp and golden and the pastry has bubbled a little. Drain on paper towels and keep warm while you fry the remainder. Serve warm or cold.

1 quantity Basic Shortcrust Pastry
(see pages 12–13)

**For the aubergine, mushroom
and coriander filling:**

2 medium aubergines/eggplants

3 tablespoons olive oil

2 shallots, finely chopped

2 tablespoons crushed
coriander seeds

225 g/1 lb. portobello mushrooms,
finely chopped

3–4 tablespoons white wine

1 medium egg, beaten

75 ml/⅓ cup double/heavy cream

60 g chopped fresh
coriander/cilantro

sea salt and freshly ground
black pepper

**For the aubergine/eggplant
garnish:**

1 small aubergine/eggplant

vegetable oil, for frying

*8 tartlet pans, 9 cm/4 inches in
diameter*

foil or parchment paper

baking beans

a deep-fryer

Makes 8

aubergine, mushroom and coriander tartlets

**These are completely vegetarian and completely delicious!
To get a really smoky flavour into the aubergines/eggplant,
try grilling them or barbecuing them whole.**

Bring the pastry to room temperature. Preheat the oven to 200°C
(400°F) Gas 6. Roll the pastry as thinly as you dare on a lightly
floured work surface, then use to line the tartlet pans. Prick the
bases, chill or freeze for 15 minutes, then bake blind following the
instructions on page 11.

Put the whole aubergines/eggplants onto a baking sheet and
bake for about 45 minutes or until soft and beginning to char.

Heat the oil in a medium saucepan and add the shallots and
coriander seeds. Cook gently for 5 minutes until soft and golden.
Stir in the mushrooms and wine and cook over high heat for
10 minutes or until all the liquid has evaporated.

Remove the aubergines/eggplants from the oven. Split them
open and scoop out the flesh. Chop the flesh coarsely and beat
into the mushroom mixture. Beat in the egg and cream. Stir in the
chopped coriander/cilantro and season well with salt and pepper.
Spoon the mixture into the tartlet shells, then bake in a preheated
oven at 190°C (375°F) Gas 5 for 15–20 minutes, or until lightly
set. Remove from the oven and serve warm.

To make the aubergine/eggplant garnish, cut the small
aubergine/eggplant into paper-thin slices using a very sharp knife.
Cut into smaller strips if necessary. Heat the oil to 180°C (350°F)
in a wok or deep-fryer, add the aubergine/eggplant and fry until
lightly browned. Drain on paper towels, then use to top the tartlets
before serving.

250 g/9 oz. Rich Shortcrust Pastry (see page 14)

For the flavoured aspic:

1 sheet of leaf gelatine

150 ml/⅔ cup light fish stock

1–2 tablespoons lemon-flavoured vodka

2 tablespoons chopped fresh chives

For the smoked salmon filling:

60 ml/¼ cup sour cream

90 g/3 oz. smoked salmon, chopped (or avruga or keta caviar)

whole chives, to garnish

a plain cookie cutter,
6 cm/2 inch diameter

2 mini bun/muffin pans, 12 holes each

foil or parchment paper

baking beans

Makes 24 tartlets

smoked salmon, vodka and sour cream tartlets

Make these pretty tartlets for a special occasion – they simply explode with fabulous flavours.

Bring the pastry to room temperature. Preheat the oven to 200°C (400°F) Gas 6.

Roll out the pastry as thinly as possible on a lightly floured work surface, then stamp out 24 circles with the cookie cutter. Use these to line the holes of the mini muffin pans. Prick the bases and chill or freeze for 15 minutes.

Blind bake the tartlet bases following the instructions on page 11.

To make the flavoured aspic, soak the leaf gelatine in cold water for 2–3 minutes until soft. Warm the fish stock, then stir in the drained gelatine until dissolved. Add the vodka. Let cool until syrupy but still pourable, then stir in the chives.

Arrange the pastry cases on a tray and add ½ teaspoon sour cream to each tartlet. Cover with a mound of smoked salmon (or a little avruga or keta caviar), then spoon in enough aspic to fill to the top of the pastry. Put in the refrigerator for 15–20 minutes to set, then garnish each one with a couple of thin chive stems. Serve immediately.

mince pies

A Christmas favourite, these delectable little treats feature pastry on the bottom, and a sort of melting piped shortbread on top of the mincemeat.

On a lightly floured surface, roll out the pastry thinly and cut out 12 rounds using the pastry cutter. Line the bun pan with the pastry, pressing the rounds into the holes. Prick the bases and chill or freeze for 15 minutes.

Meanwhile, make the Viennese paste. In a large mixing bowl and using an electric hand-whisk, cream the butter with the icing/confectioners' sugar and vanilla. It must be very, very pale, soft and light or it will not pipe. Gradually work in the flour, a tablespoon at a time, beating well between each addition. Spoon into the piping bag. (Keep this at warm room temperature or it will not pipe.)

Fill the tartlets with the mincemeat, then pipe a swirl of Viennese paste on top of each pie. Chill in the fridge for 30 minutes.

Preheat the oven to 180°C (350°F) Gas 4.

Bake the pies in the preheated oven for about 20 minutes until a pale golden brown. Let cool in the pan, then transfer to a wire rack and dust with icing/confectioners' sugar to serve. Serve warm or at room temperature – never cold!

1 quantity Rich Shortcrust Pastry (see page 14)

225 g/2 sticks unsalted butter, soft

50 g/⅓ cup icing/confectioners' sugar, sifted

1 teaspoon pure vanilla extract

225 g/1¾ cups plain/all-purpose flour

250–300 g/9–10½ oz. luxury mincemeat

a 7.5-cm/3-inch fluted pastry cutter

a 12-hole bun/muffin pan

a piping bag fitted with a star nozzle/tip

Makes 12

spiced baked apple pies

These little darlings feature a bay leaf and a sliver of
cinnamon, which act as a stalk to remind us of what is buried
under the pastry!

80 g/⅔ cup mixed
sultanas/golden raisins and
chopped dried figs

3 tablespoons dark or golden rum

30 g/2½ tablespoons soft light
brown sugar

½ teaspoon mixed/apple pie spice

125 g/1 stick softened butter,
plus extra for spreading

6 eating apples, peeled and cored

1 quantity Basic Shortcrust Pastry
(see pages 12–13)

6 small bay leaves

6 thin shards of cinnamon stick

*6 round individual ovenproof
dishes (see recipe for size)*

Serves 6

Put the sultanas/golden raisins and figs into a screw-top jar with
the rum, shake and leave to soak for at least 2 hours or overnight
(shaking occasionally). Once soaked, mix with the sugar, mixed/
apple pie spice and butter. Spoon the spiced fruit and butter mixture
into the holes in the cored apples, pressing in with the handle of a
teaspoon. Spread a little more butter over the apples. Carefully
place each apple into a round dish or ramekin in which they fit
snugly, protrude above the top edge, but don't touch the sides.

Roll out the pastry and cut out 6 circles a good bit larger than the
diameter of the dishes. Brush the rims of the dishes with a little
water and set a circle of pastry on top of each dish, gently
moulding over each apple. Press the edges of the pastry to the
rim to seal and make a tiny steam hole in the top of each pie. Use
any pastry trimmings to cut shapes to decorate the top of the pies,
then chill for 20 minutes. Meanwhile, preheat the oven to 200°C
(400°F) Gas 6.

Set the pies on a baking sheet and bake in the preheated oven
for 15 minutes to set the pastry. Reduce the temperature to
150°C (300°F) Gas 2 and stick a bay leaf and cinnamon shard
into the steam holes, then bake for a further 40 minutes until the
apples are soft but not collapsing. (If they look like they are
browning too much, cover with kitchen foil.)

1 quantity Pâte Sucrée
(see page 17)

For the passionfruit curd:

6 ripe, juicy passionfruit

freshly squeezed juice of 1 small lemon, strained

75 g/6 tablespoons butter, cubed

3 large eggs, beaten

225 g/1¼ cups sugar

For the fruit topping:

1 small fresh pineapple, peeled, cored and sliced

4 passionfruit

a fluted cookie cutter, 7.5 cm/3 inches diameter

12-hole bun/muffin pan

Makes 12 tartlets

pineapple and passionfruit curd tartlets

These exotic little treats are tangy and a little bit wicked. Remember, the more wrinkled the passionfruit, the riper the flesh inside.

Bring the pastry to room temperature before rolling out.

Cut the 6 passionfruit in half, scoop out the flesh and press through a sieve/strainer into a medium bowl to extract the juice. Add the lemon juice, butter, eggs and sugar and set over a saucepan of simmering water (or cook in a double boiler). Cook, stirring all the time, for about 20 minutes or until the curd has thickened considerably. If you are brave enough, you can cook this over direct heat, watching that it doesn't get too hot and curdle. Strain into a bowl and set aside.

Preheat the oven to 180°C (350°F) Gas 4. Roll out the pastry thinly on a lightly floured work surface and cut out 12 rounds with the cookie cutter. Line the bun/muffin pan with the pastry, pressing it into the holes. Prick the bases and chill or freeze for 15 minutes. Blind bake for 5–6 minutes without lining with beans. Let cool.

When ready to serve, fill the tartlet cases with a spoonful of passionfruit curd, then top with sliced pineapple. Cut the 4 passionfruit in half, scoop out the flesh and spoon a little, seeds and all, over each tartlet. Serve immediately before the tartlets have a chance to go soggy.

little nutmeg and bay leaf custard tarts

There's nothing quite as delicious as a real custard tart. The nutmeg is the classic flavouring here, and milk and fresh bay leaves add a mysterious musky scent to the custard.

1 quantity Pâte Sucrée (see page 17)

For the nutmeg and bay leaf custard:

600 ml/2⅔ cups whole milk

3 fresh (preferably) or dried bay leaves

6 egg yolks

75 g/⅓ cup caster/granulated sugar

1 whole nutmeg

8 loose-based tart pans, 10 cm/ 4 inches diameter (or use smaller but deeper pans and increase the cooking time)

a wire rack

Makes 8 tarts

Bring the pastry to room temperature. Preheat the oven to 200°C (400°F) Gas 6.

Roll out the pastry thinly on a lightly floured work surface and use to line the tart tins. Put these on the baking sheet and chill for 30 minutes.

To make the custard, put the milk and bay leaves into a saucepan and heat until lukewarm. Put the egg yolks and sugar into a bowl and beat until pale and creamy. Pour the warmed milk onto the yolks and stir well – do not whisk or you will get bubbles. Strain into a jug/pitcher and pour into the tart cases. Grate fresh nutmeg liberally over the surface of the tartlets.

Preheat the other baking sheet in the oven. Put the tart pans onto the preheated sheet and bake in the oven for 10 minutes. Lower the heat to 180°C (350°F) Gas 4 and bake until set and just golden – about another 10 minutes. Don't overbake as the custard should be a bit wobbly when the tarts come out of the oven.

Remove from the tart pans and let cool on a wire rack. Serve at room temperature.

traffic light tarts

A great-tasting pastry base and cheery fruit fillings turn the humble jam tart into something rather special. They are perfect for kids' parties, or simply use them to add a tasty bit of colour your afternoon tea.

Preheat the oven to 180°C (350°F) Gas 4.

Roll out the pastry on a well-floured surface until 3 mm/1/8 inch thick. Use the cookie cutter to cut discs of pastry to fit your bun/muffin pan. Not all the pastry will be needed – the excess will make another 6 or 8 tarts or can be frozen for future use.

Put the pastry discs in the pan holes and put a spoonful of jam into each one. Bake the tarts in the preheated oven for 20–25 minutes. Remove from the oven and leave to cool in the pan for 15 minutes before turning out onto a wire rack to cool completely.

The tarts are best eaten on the day of baking, or will keep for up to 2 days in an airtight container.

1 quantity Pâte Sablée (see page 17), at room temperature

For the filling:

4 dessertspoons seedless raspberry jam

4 dessertspoons apricot conserve

4 dessertspoons lemon and lime marmalade

12-hole shallow non-stick bun/muffin pan

9-cm/3½-inch round cookie cutter

Makes 12

index

recipe credits

Jordan Bourke
Broccoli and Chorizo Tart

Maxine Clark
American Pie Crust
Baked Dark Chocolate Mousse Tart
Basic Shortcrust Pastry
Chicken and Mushroom Pie
Corned Beef and Sweet Potato Pasties
Deep Dish Caramel Apple Pie
Double Cranberry and Orange Pie
Free-Form Caramelized Peach Tart
Fresh Date and Ginger Cream Pie
Goat's Cheese, Leek and Walnut Tart
Glorious Golden Fish Pie
Greek Spinach, Feta and Oregano Filo Pie
Ham and Apple Pie
Key Lime Pie
Lattice-topped Cherry Pie
Little Nutmeg and Bay Leaf Custard Tarts
Mango Curd Pavlova Pie
Mince Pies
Mississippi Mud Pie
Piggy Pies
Pineapple and Passionfruit Curd Tartlets
Potato and Parmesan Tart with Chives
Portobello Mushroom and Tarragon Tart
Pumpkin Pie
Quiche Lorraine
Rich Shortcrust Pastry
Roquefort Tart
Rough Puff Pastry
Salmon Tart
Shoofly Pie
Sour Cream Raisin Pie
Spiced Baked Apple Pies
Spicy Vegetable Samosas
Steak and Kidney Pie
Walnut Tart

Julian Day
Pâte Sablée
Pâte Sucrée
Pecan and Chocolate Tart with Maple Syrup
Tarte au Citron
Tarte Tartin
Traffic Light Tarts
Treacle Tart

Ross Dobson
Beef Pie
Chicken Pot Pie
Fresh Raspberry and Almond Tart
Herbed Courgette and Ricotta Cheese Tart
Moroccan Apple Pie
Pear, Almond and Mascarpone Tart
Snapper Pie
Swiss Chard, Feta Cheese and Egg Pie

Hannah Miles
Asparagus Tart

Miisa Mink
Blueberry Tart with Rye
Rhubarb Meringue Pie
Rhubarb Tart
Quiche with Smoked Fish
Simple Apple Tart

Isidora Popovic
Honey-Roasted Parsnip, Carrot and Shallot Tart

Laura Washburn
Mashed Potato Pie with Bacon, Leeks and Cheese
Tamale Pie

picture credits

Susan Bell
Page 77 insert

Martin Brigdale
Pages 29, 41, 56, 68 insert, 74–76, 79, 83, 108 insert, 109, 114, 118, 120, 128, 136, 138 insert, 139

David Brittain
Page 141 insert

Peter Cassidy
Pages 62, 84, 92, 97, 100 insert, 101, 110, 111 insert

Laura Edwards
Pages 71 insert, 93 insert

Tara Fisher
Pages 78 insert, 86 insert

Richard Jung
Pages 45, 63 insert, 85 insert, 87, 104 insert

William Lingwood
Page 91

Diana Miller
Page 39 insert

David Munns
Page 44 insert

Noel Murphy
Page 21

Gloria Nicol
Page 64 insert

Steve Painter
Pages 1–19, 25, 30, 33–37, 42, 46–49, 51 insert, 53, 54, 57, 58, 60 insert, 61, 65, 66, 69, 70, 73 insert, 95 insert, 96 insert, 98, 99 insert, 103 insert, 112 insert, 113, 115 insert, 116 insert, 117, 121–124, 127, 131–135, 140, endpapers

William Reavell
Pages 27, 55, 80, 81, 100 background, 125

Simon Upton
Page 40 insert

Kate Whitaker
Pages 22, 23, 26, 38, 50, 59, 72, 88, 94, 102, 105–107, 137

Polly Wreford
Page 119 insert